Harris

$15

The Ancient Stone Reading
The first steps on the Stonepath
By T L Harris

Cause all good paths are lined with stones...

...It is like tarot with stones,but not. The first stones form a
bridge to you and your life with the initial path. Then offers
you the opportunity to ask any questions you are seeking
information on. Then you learn how to draw a stone that will
help to answer any question. So, let the stones in front of you give
the knowledge you need. It is excellent with answering
question on the Health, Spirit, Romance or Empowerment and
can help you stay in the flow while addressing your mainstream issues.

Many authors, geologists, and story tellers have given description
and title to many stones throughout the planet and across time.
This book will have fifty of the most common and well understood stone
and teach you how to find answers for yourself and your friends. So like a
tarot card each stone has a meaning and each position has a meaning.
I will teach you how to cross those two and discover answer for your life,
your love and your money.

Unlike a tarot deck the book will teach you how to add to your supply of stones, as
you grow in understanding and knowledge of other stones. Here you can add a new
stone to replace the common stone at the store where you signed up for the class or
picked up this book *"The Ancient Stone Reading"*.

Thank you to all of my students

Thank you to my Grandma Daisy who taught me that All is All and we are all a part of it. She inspired me to learn that Nurture and Nature are the same thing. Thank her most of all for sharing the secret of our ancestry and the path of stone.

Thank you to my staff for putting up with all my craziness surrounding the creation of this book.

Thank you to my life partner Elizabeth, who's continued support has made this book possible.

As this book goes to press my mother and my father seem to be slipping through the other side of the veil. As I sit near them and their passing, I find myself in quiet contemplation of all that this means to me. I look at what they inspired me not to be and it worked out that I am the better part of both of their natures. I am not claiming any kind of perfection. My assertion is, I became better by doing what I liked about them. So, to them and for that, I am very grateful.

Contents

Explanation

Why do crystals, stones and minerals work?

Crystals, stones and minerals work because they are the epitome of all parts of our physical world. Color, form, magnetism and frequency all play a part but, are not the whole story, either.

Science can break down the component parts of a stone, mineral or crystal, but what they are discovering is that this is not all there is to it. Chemical and drug companies have tried to break down and use the component parts of stones, minerals and crystals for the last 150 years. They have discovered that once you remove the inert components you get a very powerful substance with (unfortunately) some very bad side effects. Science can break you down to a few dollars in minerals and some enzymes—is that all there is to you? There are more to stones also.

Stonemen, Stonewomen, Shamans, Herbalists, Monks, Medicine Men and Medicine Women have been using all of these stones, minerals, crystals and herbs since the dawn of time without adversely affecting the people they are serving. The only thing Modern Medicine has discovered is "Side Effects." Well, maybe when they stop "Practicing Medicine" and start "Doing Healing" the costs of health care will go down and the value of human life will go up.

Imagine the wonderment of primitive man or woman stumbling across a uniquely shaped, brilliantly colored crystal among a vast expanse of rock. Would it be any surprise if that person attributed mystical powers to it? Fundamental human instinct is for survival and to avoid trouble, from which springs countless taboos and superstitions. Throughout history, many minerals have been made into talisman to protect humans from wayward spirits as well as to endow humans with "super" powers.

Pictures on cave walls and clay urns show and illustrate stones used as weapons, adornments and healing tools. Historically, crystals have underpinned human development economically, technologically, and culturally. The importance of crystals links all civilizations across space and time. Until the current age of credit and hidden assets, crystals were portable forms of wealth and status. We continue to construct roads and buildings using crystalline materials such as granite and marble; concrete's rigidity and quick-setting properties depend on crystal and mineral growth and discovery.

Cultures as far back as pre-dynastic Egypt have used jewelry to celebrate human individuality. Many pictures of the ancient leaders or priests show them wearing stones, minerals and crystals all over their bodies... a walking stone layout. Good idea!

Crystals help us to interpret the past. They teach us many things about human kind's cultural heritage. Their desirability in antiquity helps us to trace trading routes between far-flung civilizations. We can monitor changing fads of gem material for decorative items and jewelry. Gem and mineral use has come in and out of fashion in every area, including medical use. Bound up with myth and magic, crystals help bring to light the different historical world views that have arisen down through the ages concerning the immutable link between humans and nature.

Throughout history, civilizations had many uses for crystals. The oldest written legends go back to the ancient times of Atlantis. It was said that the people of Atlantis were highly evolved and used crystals to channel and release the cosmic forces. One legend declares that "the sacred knowledge was abused and Atlantis was destroyed, but before it was destroyed the Wise Ones of the civilization programmed certain crystals with the information and planted them in the earth, trusting that the crystals would surface on the planet to be attracted to people who could attune their minds to receive the information stored within." In truth, we are not the first to discover that silica is great for storing information... the difference between us and the Atlanteans is that they stored their knowledge directly in natural crystals while we store ours on hard drives made of…natural crystals. Mayan, Aztec, and American Indians in the past have used crystals for diagnosis and treatment of disease. Unfortunately, most of the stone knowledge was obliterated by the US military and the Spanish conquerors and, therefore, lost to most of the world's population. Luckily, however, the knowledge **was** taught and passed from parent to child in the Medicine and Shamanic traditions and from grandparent to grandchild in the Ancient Stone Tradition.

The first known reference that gives directions for the curative use of the healing power of certain crystals comes from an Egyptian papyrus dated around 1600 BC. Beads of Lapis Lazuli, Malachite, and Red Jasper were worn around a sick person's neck so that the disease could pass through him and dissipate. The practice of placing or wearing stones on various areas of the body, thereby creating amuletic links, was only part of the repertoire of healers in history. A particularly popular medicinal method was to pulverize gems, mix them with a liquid, and drink the result—the forerunner, perhaps, of mineral water.

In 1746 Sir John Hill believed that it was the minerals that accounted for the curative powers. "Rogue" atoms of metals in some crystalline compositions are indeed responsible for the variety of colors available. Whether early civilizations knew of this link it is impossible to say, but certainly the mystical properties of gemstones were largely associated with color. When Hematite is crushed it produces a red powder: Hematite healing properties were linked with blood-related conditions.

The universal belief in the benefits of gemstone medicine began to erode in the early 16th century. One of the catalysts may have been the first systematic attempt at viewing mineralogy as a science.

In the 16th century it was discovered that the stones had a subtle effect on the body's energy systems and so were worn close to the body to bring about healing. The practice of taking gemstone powders internally continued only in high society, as might be expected, considering the high cost of the raw ingredients.

By the beginning of the 20th century, people were looking for a more scientific explanation for crystal healing. And, by the 1980s, they found it in Marcel Bogel, a respected authority on crystals, who placed the power of the crystals firmly in the scientific domain. He suggested that the key to understanding their ancient knowledge lay in the connection between the vibrations sent out by the human mind and the perfect inner structure of the crystals. It has been proven that the human mind can indeed interact with the crystal to create effects on the body, mind, and spirit.

In ancient times, 'Captured Light' was what the English called clear Quartz crystal. 'Hard Fog' is what we called white or cloudy Quartz. Obviously, if I used the ancient words you would have an even harder time understanding how to do the Stone Readings. The Latin and English 'common' names are their new ones. Though the tribal Shamans and Medicine People of the Americas as well as the holy Druids of Europe and the Vedics of Asia knew of these stones by different names, they all had practical and spiritual uses for the stones, crystals and minerals. Amethyst, for example, had many other names but, the only difference in it's description of it's healing power was the way it it was said.

So, whether Stone Reading was invented last week or has existed (as my grandmother told me) before women knew stones were pretty and certainly before men knew to get their woman one...let's have some fun with Ancient Stone Readings.

High above a portion of the Smithsonian Institute in Washington DC is a memorial series of reliefs. This one depicts and honors all those who participate in digging minerals out of the ground to keep our society moving.

The Stone Reading...

In preparation for the reading, you should be in a place where the recipient or you will not be distracted or disturbed by what is going on around you. There should be a surface that you can put the stones on. If the surface is the ground then lay a blanket or scarf down to put the stones on. It is best (especially in the beginning of your path) to have a space that has been purified with sage or by whatever method best suits your beliefs... prayer works well too. As you move more and more into the work, you will be ready to do a reading in a train station if needed. Until you are used to feeling the guiding light, the hand of God, the positive flow, the Great Spirit, or the Allness, you should prepare the space as I have described.

Place yourself in a position that allows you to face the person getting the reading. This is more important than would first appear. The stones form a bridge between the recipients' life and your insight.

The reading begins with you holding the bag of stones against you, just above your navel. Then clear and bless the stones for the person you are doing the reading for. While you are blessing them, gently tumble or roll the stones inside your bag. (The previous should take far less than a minute.)

Then hand the bag of stones to the person you are reading for (Q= questioner). Then tell Q to remove five stones from the bag and lay them out in a straight line between you and Q, from your right to your left. While Q is doing that, close your eyes and ask that you be granted a helpful and perfect connection to Q so that your information can be for Q's highest and best good. Keep doing this until Q has finished drawing the stones and has laid them out in whatever order feels right to her.

The First Position...

... is always on your right, Q's left. It signifies the energy Q was born with or the energy she came through to take on physical form. It was here Q began her transition through to the first few years of her life.

The Second Position...

... is next to the first and working across to your left. It signifies what was generally going on with Q in her next phase of growth (toddler, childhood and early adolescence).

The Third Position...

... is in the direct middle of the five stones and signifies the energy, lessons characteristics and/or aspirations of the teenage years.

The Fourth Position...

... is how Q used the previous energies to help formulate his plans for breaking away from her birth family and to begin to act as an agent of her own interests (usually associated with the young adult years).

The Fifth Position...

... is the near past to present and indicates what outcomes Q is bringing about with the energy that personifies her now.

After you have finished with the description of Q's fifth position, ask "Do you feel like we have formed a bridge?" or "Does this sound like I've correctly described your life to this point?" You will get all kinds of answers that will signify a yes to the question, but if Q tells you no... simply end the reading. However, if Q says anything that is not a "NO"—which will usually be the case—ask, "Do you want to have more information about anything I've covered so far, or do you have another question?"

The Sixth Position...?

... What? But you only drew five stones! This position is only drawn if Q is asking about the future. It is irresponsible, reckless, and rude to pull the future stone unless asked. Too many things, including the reading you are doing for Q, could have an effect on her future. It is NOT okay and it is applying the path of "Pain", not the path of Service to give this piece without being asked. NO, you should not ask a person if she "would like to know what the future holds." Q must request the information of her own volition.

How to handle a Question...

If Q asks a question about any or all of the five stones that you have laid out for her, do your best to answer it without pulling another stone. Close your eyes, think about the question, the stone(s) and the associated position(s). See if any additional information occurs to you to say to Q. If you need to draw a stone to answer a question about the original five stones, have her draw a stone from the bag and place it in front of the stone or area she had a question about or in front of the two to five stones she had a question about (in front in this case meaning between you and Q). Read the description of the stone (if needed) and/or reflect on what that stone could mean in regards to Q's question, and then give her that information as it applies.

I just have a quick question...

   Here's what to do if Q has a question not related to the original five stones you read this time or if you have recently done another stone reading for him or he comes at another time and says "I Just Have A Quick Question." YOU pull three stones from the bag and lay them out in a row between you and Q. This could be on the same table you just did the reading on or the palm of your hand, as long as it is between you and the person.

The middle position is the Questioner & it is the First stone that is drawn...

   … who is she in this question, what control does she have over it, what is her energy about it. It could be some of what is answered by the stone that is in the middle position...or all of the above.

The Second position is the SET UP...

   … again, the first spot to the stone reader's right is the token stone of the situation surrounding the question or what led to the question.

The answer is the third position...

   Consider this stone carefully, read the description of the stone and look at the question or the situation. Take notes, if necessary, before giving an answer.

   I've been doing this long enough that sometimes I simply look at the three stones and know exactly what I need to say to Q. Sometimes, even though I have been doing this for a very long time, I pull three stones and am completely dumbfounded as to their connection to the questioner or question. So, I start sharing everything I know about each of the stones and almost always Q starts "filling in the blanks" for us both. The answer stone is sometimes the most difficult to interpret, because it is the stone from which you derive the answer to Q's question.

   In general, I don't like answering a 'quick' question for someone that I haven't done a five stone spread for within the previous two weeks—I don't feel I have a proper understanding of the energies surrounding the person's life at the moment—but this is not a hard and fast rule. I am not telling you not to do it—just that doing a one question reading gives Q a superficial response

   I developed this technique when I got signed onto a psychic party circuit and was asked to do readings in three to five minutes. To me this is like going to the naturopath and asking if vitamins are good for me...and only giving her five minutes to answer because that's all I can pay for.

   Since you now understand that the five stone layout is age-defined, if you need help to answer the

Just a Question

quick question, try to determine or even ask Q's age. As with the five to six stone reading, sometimes the answer is best interpreted based on age. If needed, go to the section on the stone that you have drawn to the five stone descriptions. For example, you are being asked a question from a teenager, then you should probably look at the stone definition in the third position; if you are reading for a fifty year old, you may want to read the stone in the fifth position, and if you are answering a question about an infant by a parent, the first position.

What can I use this method for?

I have used this method to evaluate stocks for my portfolio, companies I wanted to buy or buy into, products and their growth potential, dates and times to do or not to do something. I have used this to look at the health of myself and my clients. It's been used to develop treatment protocols or decide whether to take someone's advice. You can use this to decide whether or not to enter into a business or personal relationship and/or if the gamble will be worth it.

I can honestly say the stones have never been wrong... If only I had listened to them with the same percentage. The stones are so accurate, I am sometimes afraid to ask the question because I fear they will not give me the answer I want to hear.

I have been doing this for a very long time, please do not expect to have the same skill or accuracy with the stone reading as I enjoy. The first time you pick up a hammer, you may smack your thumb or fingers before you hit the nail... it may take you awhile to get used to this tool so you too can NAIL it.

How do I use this method when people aren't involved?

First of all, people are always involved; they might not be sitting in front of you. And, energy is energy. You could do a reading for someone in another state or about an issue that is personal to you. You simply do the reading or ask the question as if you were doing it for someone in the same room with the only exception being that you draw the stones yourself.

How do I read the stones for a couple?

Have the couple sit in separate chairs directly facing you. Both people draw two stones each (stone placement #2 &3) and then put them in a row in front of them. You then have them reach into the bag together to draw a stone that would go in between the two stones they drew individually(Stone placement #1) to represent the reason and/or the energy behind how they got together.

The first stones you read are each of their drawn stones closest to the middle stone (the stone in position #2) and these represent the largest component or amount of energy each one brings to their shared path. Next read the stone furthest away from the middle stone (stone In position #3). This is what the drawer of the stone gets out of being in the relationship. If either or both ask or elude to wanting to know "their" future, the answer would be based on what you have disclosed to them in this reading; one or both draw another stone and put it in front of the original two stones they drew. If one wants to know the future but the other doesn't, then they have to resolve this before you continue.

When talking to people about a shared life path, it is important to mention the potential dark side of a trait: for example, Amethyst can indicate someone is being very protective... which also can manifest as being controlling. The creative energy can also indicate someone may be "creating drama" if they don't have another outlet or are prone to starting projects and never finishing them. Be mindful of not just telling people the warm fuzzy parts of their readings but also don't spend a great deal of time on the negative—mention it and then move on. They will ask more about it if they need to.

Since you are sitting across from this couple, you have one on your left and one on your right. Depending on the amount of time they have allowed you for the reading, you can answer the questions in the same way as described in this book or if time allows, go through each of the 12 areas of human expression: Occupation, Intimacy, Physical, Family, Emotional, Mental, Spiritual, Social, Education, Financial, Gifts, Calling. The person on your right draws from the bag goes on the right: it represents what the person on the right brings into that area for their mutual benefit. Do the same for the person on the left. Then, you draw a stone for the stone that goes in the middle, which is the outcome or result of their shared energy. A a complete couple's reading takes me an hour to do.

Kids, partners and other pilgrims ...

Sometimes parents want to know what the future holds for their children or what's currently up with their children. OR, business people want to know who to be in partnership with. OR, pet owners want to know the traits of their pet, OR, you have just finished doing one of the other readings and someone says I need more information on what you said about ___. Before you begin this do a perception check with the questioner. Ask them if they want you to see if you perceive a little more or are they after a complete and thorough answer? If they are just want a little more and you have the information and want to share it, tell them. If they want a complete answer, here's what I do for these situations. I use the string method, which is laying the stones one at a time in a row between Q and you, instead of from left to right. The first stone I draw tells me about the core personality of the child, partner, or pet as it relates to the question. If the questioner has a very specific question, I pull a stone and interpret the stone's meaning in regard to the question. Or, I go through the twelve areas. Each stone that I draw is laid in a line below the first stone.

I spend an entire day explaining the complexities and ramifications of the 12 areas of human experience. So, I'm not going to try to be as complete about this now. I will only share and explain what is relevant to your use of the stones and this type of layout. The most important element that many people lose sight of is when each stone is drawn, the information is only as it relates to the question. To keep this in your (and the questioner's) mind have them write down on a scrap of paper, their question. Then each time (before) you or they draw a stone have them look at the question then draw the stone.

When you are doing this reading, Explain to them what each of the positions and stone meanings are, this will also help you interpret the combined meaning. Those positions are

Q = Whatever or whomever the question is about.

E = Emotional, What are the emotions around the Q?

M = Mental, What are the thoughts, reasons or excuses around the Q?

S = Spiritual, What is the soul connection and faith relating to Q?

P = Physical, How is the Q present and evident in moving forward with Q?

F = Family, How is Q intertwined in the whole situation.

I = Intimacy, How important and close is Q?

S = Social, How is Q connected to the sphere of influence of other people concerning the situation?

O = Occupation, What affect will Q have on the world's perception of what or who you are?

Ed = Education, What, if any, is the learning curve that will be created by Q?

Fn = Financial, How will Q affect the resources available?

G = Gifts, What will Q bring out in those around them?

C = Calling, How will Q create a better realization of the dream of this situation?

The Ten Stone Method

An alternative method of using the stones for a reading is very similar (in appearance) to what is referred to as Celtic Cross in tarot. However each position has a slightly different meaning than that of the tarot's Celtic Cross.

1) How Q sees herself or the marriage/partnership or corporation.
2) How others perceive Q, or her marriage/ partnership, or corporation.
3) Energy of the recent past relating to Q's situation.
4) Significant event(s) of the recent past relating to Q's situation.
5) Energy of the next event relating to Q's situation.
6) Next event relating to Q's situation.
7) Energy of Q's involvement in the situation, marriage/ partnership or corporation.
8) Contributing factor to Q's marriage/ partnership, corporation, or situation.
9) Energy of the other person(s) involved or any other contributing factor to Q's marriage/ partnership, corporation, or situation.
10) Outcome to Q's question about her marriage/ partnership, corporation, or situation.

Situation Spread

The Stonepath... a beginning

There is a lot more to learn about being a Stone Man or Stone Maiden and a world more to learn about lapidology. This is only the first step along this magical, ancient Stonepath. Use this book as your primer into the world of stones, gems, crystals, and minerals. Further along, I offer up more information on the Stonepath and the scientific faith of Lapidology. I will offer you a number of the most common stones, gems, crystals, and minerals, some of my "easy to find" favorites, and a way for you to add a few to your collection to make them yours.

On the stones themselves I share a good amount of the information I possess. I will provide brief but significant descriptions of these stones and how I would read them in any one of the given positions.

Before I begin the stone section, I would like to give you a little information on which to hang your faith. Here is a tale that was told to me, one that could have happened in any town with any group of children...of course this happened a very long time ago....

...in a land that no longer exists on a continent that was pulled apart and swallowed by the great sea at the time of the great break. This Great Land was known for its mastery of the elements, the way it lit up the night and brightened the daily lives of everyone that shared the domain. But before it came into its greatness it also had a beginning. In the beginning there were a number of settlers. One of these settlers had two great gifts—one for finding unusual stones and the other for helping children who were, as he was once, without a family.

Erastis was a trader in the beginning, before he became a merchant. He learned that people liked his sparkly stones and, almost by accident, discovered they would give him what he needed if he traded one of his stones with them.

THE BEGINNINGS OF LAPIDOLOGY

The children of the land helped Erastis break and sort the stones he brought home in his huge cart. The children were working (and playing) one day when the oldest noticed that whoever was working with the sparkly red stone was getting mean, ornery, and angry. Over the next two or three days, he had most of the children take turns on that pile. They were all affected in a similar way. So he told all the children what he had noticed. Then Tazshe said, "I only do my mind work (what we call homework) in the blue-green stone chair because it is easier there." The oldest girl, Omlie, said, "I always put the statue of the goddess in the room with a new or upset little one because it calms the baby down." Then she mused over whether it was the goddess statue that brought comfort or the pink, white, and black stone it was made out of. They all decided they would play with the stones and see what they did.

Many of the stones didn't cause any immediate reaction, but some did. Some changed a person in a short time and others took days...but the person holding the stone hardly ever noticed the change. It was the children around the other boy or girl that noticed. Then one of them thought of a (Really Good) idea.

One of them suggested they put some stones in other people's pockets to see what happened. They all thought that would be fun.

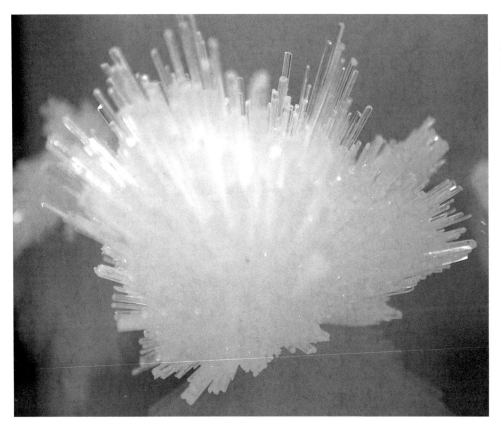

The local people would gather, once in a while, to talk and share a meal in a big, open, grass-covered common some distance from the village. The children thought it would be fun to try the experiment there. Mikdo (the oldest boy of 11) decided that he would be the one to carry the stones, so he put a lot of small pieces of the stones in a double leather bag and then they began their journey to the common. By mid-morning the stones were having an effect on Mikdo, but luckily the children soon arrived at the tall grass.

He passed out the stones and the children began to walk over the common. They managed to put some in, on, or around many people. The youngest, being a little less patient (and perhaps a little more timid), dropped all of his stones into a very large man's pouch and ran off. The children were just about to the point of thinking that this game wasn't any good at all when they suddenly noticed that one woman who had one certain stone seemed friendlier with the people, but that they themselves were fighting even more than usual, and the men had started hitting each other... Soon the experiment wasn't fun anymore.

Erastis received several blows trying to stop his friends from hitting each other. Mikdo came over and confessed to Erastis what he and the other children had done. Erastis gave Mikdo and the other children a disappointed look, then turned and told the people to start searching for the red stone. Once the fury of the people dissipated, it was decided that the *stones, gems, crystals, and minerals needed to be better understood.*

Erastis became the first Lapidologist. Maybe he wasn't the greatest to have lived, but he was the first to document for the purpose and safety of society stones, minerals, crystals, and gems...more of this story is coming in a separate book.

TODAY... all we have left of this great scientific faith, following our way of life is the jeweler's trick to sell more stones and gems by classifying certain ones as "birthstones." This isn't to say that birthstones are not significant—they are very significant. However, the list jewelers use just happens to be comprised of their most valuable stones and is missing another 156 stones, gems, or minerals.

Another fact and factor to question is "Why **are** we affected by a stones, gems, or crystals." The answer is fairly easy to explain:

You have a magnetic pole that runs from the soles of your feet to the top of your head. You also have a current pole or equator that is created by your breathing. Charges that run through your body and blood flow are constantly created by the forces of friction and resistance in your physical form. Your aura mostly runs side to side, parallel to the ground, arches over your head, and tightly by or around your center of gravity.

So it shouldn't surprise you that the earth, our solar system, and the galaxy have magnetic and current poles also. Kirlian photography has captured this in humans, plants, and animals. If you could see auras (and some can), you would see colorful bands around the body. Those bands are like your own personal Aurora Borealis that can be seen in nature. What causes the bands to quiver is the current or electrical poles of the planet and your body; the Asian culture calls it your Chi. The great teachers and thinkers of our past have mentioned "our connection" to each other. It is the magnetic and current fields that allow us to be connected.

The stones have developed (over millions of years) through being pushed and pulled by the attraction to the electrical and magnetic planetary influences. So, as a general rule, stones are more magnetic, whereas crystals are more current- or frequency-based. Now, because you and the stones, gems, crystals, and minerals all developed on this planet, they interact with your fields and energies to help to steer you in directions that are beneficial to you.

Let's discuss this from an anthropological point of view. Part of being a successful human being has always meant BEING able to identify and capitalize on "What Works." I could write a book on the ancient and current attraction to stones, gems, crystals, and minerals by all the peoples of the earth (and I am going to include more on this in a future book). The earliest evidence of human dwellings or civilizations demonstrates that stones, gems, crystals, and minerals were as much a part of their lives as they are part of ours today. They wore them as beads or in a bag around their necks and we wear them as a brooch, earrings, or a ring. Although most of us no longer carve idols to speak with the Gods, none of our electronics would work without crystals, metals, or minerals...in fact, we would die without minerals. Obviously "What Works" both then and now is our connection to gems, stones, crystals, and minerals.

The way this book is structured is not as a textbook. Although I include many facts, the descriptions here are not as exhaustive as they will be in successive books. We have attempted to make the photography in this book as attractive as possible and to photograph stones that you are likely to find in your local store. We didn't go to the richest collections or to the finest museums to take photographs of "one of a kind" examples. Your accurate understanding of what is available and your understanding of the stones' work in your life is what is important to me.

Part of the proceeds from the sales of this book will go to further the resurrection of the ancient teachings of Lapidology and the Ancient Stone Path. This book is intended to help get you started on the awesome path of a Stoneworker or to help to introduce you to the concepts of Lapidology (both the scientific and the spiritual connection of stones). This is supposed to be fun. So grab a bunch of friends and enjoy doing and reading "The Ancient Stone Readings."

Agate,
Blue Lace

Agates in general are best regarded as "A GATE." They are portals, openings, doorways, or hallways that lead to other spaces you are not currently in. Depending on the position of the agate in the reading and/or the question being asked, it can also mean that you need to find a portal, opening, doorway, or hallway. Agates are especially useful in opening chakra points and meridians on the body during stone layouts for healing purposes.

When George Swanson discovered Blue Lace Agate on his farm in Namibia, he first called it the gem of ecology because of its swirling sky-like blues and whites. This is an environmental stone. It is connected to the sign Pisces and the Element of Air and is most commonly allied with the Throat Chakra.

Blue Lace Agate signifies communication. It can be used to help someone who is blocked in speaking or "saying what they mean." This would be a great jewelry gift for someone who does a lot of public speaking. A large piece would be very useful in a meeting room, class space, or convention center.

With its subtle protective nature (strong Guardian Angel connection) it helps to keep people grounded in their faith and offers a feeling of restful peace.

Blue Lace Agate has been used to heal hotness or swelling of bones (Rheumatoid Arthritis) and has been applied to the throat and breathing as it relates to allergies or asthma. People with frequent headaches have found agate to be helpful.

The First Position...
...You came into this world as a communicator and probably cried really well as a baby. You may have come in with a message and/or knowledge to impart...regardless, as a young child you could share your truth and explain it better than anyone around you, and certainly better than those in your peer group.

The Second Position...
…You spoke your truth as best you could as a young child, and you could be very soothing to those around you. You may have even liked to sing. You also didn't mind telling someone if something was wrong.

The Third Position...
…You used your voice as a tool to get attention from those around you. Hopefully this was a positive use because your voice carried weight and always caused a reaction. If your voice was not expressed positively then you may have had a rough time as a teenager. You

also had a very hard time being around someone who was being picked on and may have chosen to "step in" and protect the person.

The Fourth Position...

...Your emerging voice was very poignant and straightforward and hopefully you found yourself in a position of respect. You may have been regarded by many as being "opinionated" or forceful. Yet your intention was always what was best for all. You may be an excellent peacemaker, able to cool situations with words rather than deeds.

The Fifth Position...

...You are coming to grips with all that has happened in the past and are creating or have created resolution in areas that seemed to be too different at first. You are or are becoming able to speak your truth...that is to speak of what you believe with clarity and be very precise when necessary.

The Sixth Position...?

...You are going to be in a position of defending yourself with your voice, and/or the words you have spoken may be brought into question. If you stay on track with what you believe to be accurate you can rest assured that the outcome will be to your long term benefit.

Agate,

Moss

Moss Agate is associated with nature, agriculture, and new beginnings. It is also associated with nature spirits, bringing Earth energy into its healing. The gentle, nurturing energy of Moss Agate encourages the user to appreciate and enjoy each moment on Earth, and assists the planet in its healing as well. Moss Agate is considered a "birthing" crystal that can assist midwives in their work. Moss Agate helps to release old habits and promote forgiveness. It also attracts wealth and abundance, improves self-esteem and helps to calm and release fears. Moss Agate also comforts and soothes emotional wounds.

Moss Agate is mostly brecciated and is a variety of chalcedony, a fibrous crypto-crystalline variety of quartz with other minerals in it. The clearer chunks or parts can be nearly as hard as quartz (7 hardness,) yet the cloudy area can be as soft as 5. Found mostly in the US and Canada, some great specimens have come from Europe and South America.

As with any other agate, this is "A GATE" to something new, natural, or simply a new beginning.

The First Position...
...You are the new thing that arrived in your family that necessitated adjustment following your birth. When people held you (as a baby), you made people look to create "new" in their lives.

The Second Position...
... As a young child you helped to find new ways to discover the world. You may have been the first person in your family to get to know the neighbors.

The Third Position...
...You were seriously into what was the newest and coolest thing and made friends quickly in junior high and high school. The search for new experiences could have led you down paths that weren't good, or you really loved the new experience that learning and education offered.

The Fourth Position...

... It was important for you to find a way or path out and away from your childhood and teenage years. Your attraction to nature is a source of strength for you.

The Fifth Position...

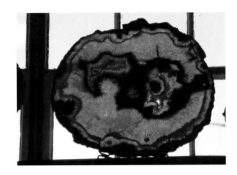

…You are about to begin ANEW physically. Changes are or have just started to occur. Walk through this gate with grace and ease into this newness or the universe will pull you through it. If you have been engaging in destructive physical habits you should probably go have some test done, or maybe this is just a reminder that you are about to cross a doorway physically that you won't be able to get back from... In other words QUIT the bad habit.

The Sixth Position...?

... What stands before you are three gates. One you have to work to get through, one you are going to slide through by leaning to one direction, or to get through the third, you will slightly change course and go down that one. (You may need to pull three more stones to get an idea of which gates they are and the paths they lead to, but wait till they ask).

Amber

`   Amber coats, covers, and protects and its energy is enveloping. Great if you want to be guarded, not so much if you are seeking freedom. Wonderful as a blocking or stopping stone for Talisman work. Helps you to focus intellectually and avoid distraction mentally.

The above doesn't really describe how wonderful this stone is. Amber acts as a guardian and protector so it is great for young children when you can't be with them. It stands in the gap for you so that you can't get taken advantage of. Since you can't reach out and pull back at the same time, It is excellent for holding you in a position you are comfortable with.

The First Position...

... You were a comfort to everyone who held as a baby and they should have felt reminded of the universe's love for them by holding you. You may have been a fussy baby and that needed to be held a lot.

The Second Position...

… Being a toddler and adolescence may have been disturbing to you because of all the changes inherent in the process of growing through this period of any human development. You may have clung to those people and things that were comfortable to you, until you were comfortable in the new situation.

The Third Position...

… You may have perceived yourself as a watcher or wall flower during your teenage years, while others felt you were a great friend and very comfortable to be around.

The Fourth Position...

... You had a hard time leaving home. You have a hard time venturing out or being risky. You are a blessing and a balance to the world around you. You are capable of reminding people what is good in the now and warn them about the risks of change.

The Fifth Position...

… You have been putting on the brakes a little too much. You need to remind yourself nothing ventured nothing gained. You have some choices and need to make one.

The Sixth Position...?

... You can coast for a while; no need to continue to push your way through. More effort is not needed and all it will do is tire you out. Relax and let things settle. You have been so busy, you haven't had time to address small things... coast for about 60 to 90 days, watch what and where things fall. Let them fall. You can charge in and straighten or clean things up later. Rest and be at ease for the moment.

AMETHYST

Amethyst has, for many years, been the Crown Chakra stone and a doorway to access higher knowledge. It enhances psychic abilities and cleanses the synapses of the brain. Amethyst helps to pierce erroneous thinking and helps you to cut through drama and untruth. As an anchor stone for home or business, it moves you to higher frequencies in the physical, spiritual, emotional, and ethereal levels. The healing energy of amethyst is for blood and brain disorders. It is a great stone for helping to move people through low self-worth issues.

When Amethyst is pulled for....

The First Position...

...You came in with a strong connection to the higher realms of masters, teachers, and guides.

The Second Position...

...You perceived your environment very well as a young child.

The Third Position...

... Since your teenage years you have been hard to fool, and you have the ability to understand situations better than most people.

The Fourth Position...

...You are probably one of the first to notice when something is over and done with. You move through most of life's situations knowing what you and others should do and have felt pretty comfortable with this since you were of age.

The Fifth Position...

...The outcome of all that you have come through is to be in a position of mentorship and offer your world a new coach, teacher, priest, and/or best friend.

The Sixth Position...?

...You are being offered a path of ascension. If you resist or try to force it, this path can be painful. If you accept and move into it with the idea of being of service, it can be a warm and comfortable transition.

ANGELITE

This blue and white stone was discovered in Peru in 1987. It has a strong connection with etheric levels, acting as a balancing agent between the etheric and physical bodies. It enhances communication, both sending and receiving, by raising the state of conscious awareness. It promotes peace and, through the sense of connectedness, "brotherhood" in the world. The industry definition of angelite— "A trade name for a semi-transparent, light blue-grey Anhydrite marketed as a gem material"—does little to explain the feelings of peace and protection or the ease of spiritual awakening this stone helps to provide.

Angelite is a great stone to use in a corporation or a non-profit or volunteer organization, as it helps to promote brotherhood and/or a sense of connectedness.

If someone has had a disturbing childhood experience, angelite can be a bridge toward restoring that sense of safety that was missing from her early years.

While meditating with this stone, it is highly likely that your "inner voice" will become more audible, or that you will receive a greater sense of discernment. This stone is often given as gifts to young priests or rabbis. Due to its relative softness and resulting ease in carving, it was often made into fetishes and other shapes. It can be found in its white or blue form in every major region of the world. This stone works well in combination with other stones and crystals.

The First Position...

...You were never pleased with conflict and were always trying to bridge people or help them get along ... or rather that is how you started in this life.

The Second Position...

...You were probably the first one to make friends in your family and/or tried to step in to make "peace" whenever there was an argument or disturbance.

The Third Position... ... Although it could be said that any teenager wants to belong, your friends were more a place for you to find rest and peace, and you may have found yourself as the counselor for your group as a teenager.

The Fourth Position...
...This indicates that you may have or needed to escape from your childhood rather than just moving out. OR, you may have found a new person/group to fix, whether that was/is a spouse, new friends, co-workers.

The Fifth Position...
...Angelite in this position indicates that you are now or you are becoming a diplomat in your sphere of influence. You could also be accused of being a "bridge builder" of opposing sides.

The Sixth Position...?
...If Angelite is drawn as the future stone, it indicates that you will need to either become the person that is expressed in position five or find that person. Our lives are full of intersections and crossed paths. Sometimes life may be like a stroll through a lovely garden and other times more like a fender-bender. Be mindful of your actual **and** your non-physical intersections and be sure to look both ways before you proceed.

Apache Tear

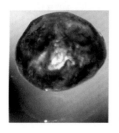

Apache Tear comes from galactic particulate that fell to the earth and changed the soil around it to the matrix that it is now. The matrix that Apache Tear is found in is neither volcanic nor pumice (hardened volcanic powder). The matrix was ground and mixed with honey and Jojoba Cactus and used to heal organ and flesh wounds from the inside out. (An alternative to honey was the cactus Agave, and an alternative to the Jojoba was Aloe ...and was sometimes preferred).

Apache Tear is excellent for piercing into deep emotional issues and assists in releasing those deep emotional issues. It spiritually aids in forgiveness of self and others and works through the Root Chakra. Mentally speaking, Apache Tear leads us away from erroneous thinking.

Although technically classified as a type of glass known as obsidian, it has some interesting variances. While glass has a hardness of 3–5 and most obsidians have a hardness of 5–5.5, Apache Tear has a hardness of 6+. That would explain why the Apache and others used it as arrow and spear heads. Apache Tear also has a radiant magnetic signature, which may have something to do with it having come from stars.

Much of the stories and folklore around Apache Tear is wrong and silly. For example, most of the textbooks and other written sources claim that obsidian is a direct result of volcanic activity. In the case of Apache Tear, that is clearly wrong since the matrix Apache Tear is found in neither volcanic rock nor in pumice.   Lastly, there is a lot of volcanoes around the world (both live and long dead). Why hasn't Apache tear or something like it (clear glass nodules) appeared else where?

"Apache tears–dark gray to nearly black, pebble-sized glass nodules, most of which have greatest dimensions ranging between two and four centimeters, that occur as remnants within or weathered out of light gray perlite. (Perlite, apparently derived from obsidian as the result of hydration involving meteoric water, is a light gray rock made up of concentrically fractured fragments.) Many apache tears in the marketplace are from Maricopa and Pinal counties in Arizona."
http://www.cst.cmich.edu

The First Position...

... Apache Tear signifies that you were a quiet baby and that your connection to the outer world was very limited to a close proximity to your parents. At first you didn't like to be held by anyone other than them and only others as you become familiar. You probably came into this world to help build tight bonds of community.

The Second Position...

…Your natural shyness (or that is what many would call it) continued (or continues). You bond to individuals deeply but not quickly, and they must be around you for a while before you do.

The Third Position...

…You didn't make friends quickly in high school, even if you were popular; you only allowed a certain number of people into your tribe. Loosing close relationship was very hard for you. To see a friend move away or at the passing of a close elder was, and may still be, very difficult for you.

The Fourth Position...

... As you move(d) into your young adult years, you found the pulling away from friends and family a very difficult adjustment. And it still bothers you that those relationships haven't come back together. Your nature is to care about a group of people and to be intimate with a tribe. It is easier for you to share yourself with a group than it is with any one individual.

The Fifth Position...

…Now is the time for you to release old issues that are holding you back. You are now able to feel the release that comes from forgiveness and move forward with the wings of peace and joy lifting you higher and higher.

The Sixth Position...?

…You are now or you soon will become a leader of your tribe. We all have a tribe: we just don't call it that—we call it a group of friends or a sphere of influence. Whatever you call it, you will soon have or are now moving through a chance to become one of its leaders. Consider each decision carefully because you are choosing for more than just you. RE-think about whatever choices you have made in the last month because you may need to turn them around for the greater good of your tribe.

Apophyllite

    Apophyllite forms in cubic and pyramidal structures. This stone creates a conscious connection between the physical and spiritual realms. It is primarily used to facilitate astral travel and to channel information from astral realms. It can also assist with dream recall.

    Ancient Vedics and healers of India, medicine men on the North American and South American continents used the substance we now call apophyllite as an aid to someone who wasn't sleeping well or had nightmares... Science has now confirmed a link between disturbing or poor sleep to a lack of potassium... Guess what apophyllites primary mineral is? K or Potassium. The actual formula is $KCa_4Si_8O_{20}(F,OH) \cdot 8H_2O$. In it's best or clearest form it resembles an Ice cube that doesn't melt. However, it may fall apart if you leave it in water or it dries out. Potassium/Calcium/Silica/Oxygen creates a link between the higher-self/ spiritual and the mental understanding which opens you to receive those spiritual messages.

    Where to get this awesome stone, isn't all that difficult. Go to the store where you got this book and get it there. There are about 50 mines in the United states that you can drive/walk up to, maybe another 50 that you need to be a more aggressive traveler to find in the USA. There are easily that many more in the rest of the world (don't go to any mines outside of the USA without a guide AND permission). Some of the best , most available, specimens come out of India but, Germany, Canada, Norway, Japan, Scotland, Ireland and Brazil also have good specimens.

The First Position...

... You were probably a baby that people admired because of the depth and wisdom within your eyes as they held you. You were probably a delight at nap time and began sleeping through the night at an early age. You could probably drift off to an easy or peaceful sleep almost anywhere as you were growing up.

The Second Position...

... You were probably easier to get to take a nap than other children and got very recharged by having one. Even now, you are probably one of those people who would be extremely benefited by a quick cat nap. While you were growing up, people were amazed at how much understanding or maturity they saw in you.

The Third Position...

... While you were growing up, people were amazed at how much understanding or maturity they saw in you. You were probably like a counselor to your friends and others because of your gift of deep knowledge and understanding.

The Fourth Position...

... You have a strong spiritual core and needed to find the space and grace to develop the gifts you came in with. You didn't shune anyone like your friends or family but you may have had to go away for a (short or long) while to find that spiritual core. You may have moved back to the same neighborhood you grew up in or helped to form the spiritual community where you now live.

The Fifth Position...

... You need to reconnect with your spiritual core. You have become disconnected enough to even wonder if there really is a soul or spirit. Where physicality is reality. Don't let the mirror fool you. Carrying a piece of lapis lazuli might help with this.

The Sixth Position...?

... If you do not like the way things are going, now is the time to connect with the Astral plane, through God, Allah, Buddha, Angels, Faeries or any other part of the Allness you feel connected to and renegotiate your agreement. Lay it out the way you like or would like to see it improved, then accept it and begin living.

ARAGONITE

Aragonite is like planting roots, this stone prepares one for growth and change. It assists with manifestation into the physical plane. Aragonite is good for focus and concentration and prepares one for meditation or the job at hand. Stimulates bone growth & strength. Found everywhere, Gem form available Named in 1797 for the type locality, Molina de Aragón, Spain.

One curiosity is how this material can be both crystalline and stone and yet have the same name. Although it is true that they share a common chemistry, the stone varieties are not found with crystal or vise versa. Ruby, garnet, aquamarine, amethyst and citrine (amongst others) are found with their matrix attached in substantial amounts. The hardness of quartz is 7.5 anywhere that it is found in the world. Neither the hardness nor the material compositions are the same with aragonite.

Our own testing show that the crystal version puts out more frequency, while the stone is magnetic. Yet, the harmonics are within the same range. Which (along with how Carbon, calcium and oxygen affect humans) is where we get the conclusion that this would be very good to assist with overall concentration and help people be less "scattered" in their daily lives.

Formula $CaCO_3$
Calcium 40.%
Carbon 12.% C 43. % CO_2
Oxygen 47.96 % O
Hardness:3½ – 4

http://www.skullis.com/pro/4800376.html

The First Position...
... You made your parents and others focus on what is essential to keep the physical form going and growing. Being around you may have inspired people to improve their lives in a practical way and or at least give the practical side of life more attention.

The Second Position...
... You could probably be counted on or relied upon your whole life. Asking you to do something was almost a guarantee that it would get done. You probably where "very" grown up even at a young age and don't remember playing very much or having much of a childhood.

The Third Position...

… You probably had your life planned out by the time you were a teenager. You may have been a very good student or were at least working on your future all the way through high school. You may not have had a plan to rule the world but you at least had a plan to be ruling your world.

The Fourth Position...

… You needed to put all of your plans into motion and set out to get that done as early as you could... Maybe you waited till you were 18 to move away from your family and childhood but whenever that was; it was about recreating the world that made sense to you. Not necessarily in a spiteful or conceited way, but the path and direction you thought best for you.

The Fifth Position...

… You are or are about to bring things to ground level, back to practical. And it is you that is making the decision to do so. You know you need to make things work again... to repair or replace whatever isn't working so that your life can become more pleasant and productive for you.

The Sixth Position...?

… Things are about to be brought to ground level, back to practical. You need to have things work again... to have repaired or replaced whatever isn't working so that your life can become more pleasant and productive for you. While some of this may seem uncomfortable, take a deep breath and simply allow what must happen to happen.

Atlantisite

...Atlantisite comes from Australia and allows us to move through our inherited Karma or Issues. Even back to Atlantis and Lemuria. It creates a cocoon around anyone meditating with it, to allow them to transfer into the beautiful butterfly of their awakening and helps us all move forward.

In the christian Bible it talks about "the sins of the father are passed onto the children for the next 7 generations" and bad habits abound in some families. Atlantisite help break up your predispositions and allow you to move forward with your motivations, being no longer bound by inherited bad habits.

Stones mostly radiate magnetics, while crystals cause frequencies. Because this combination creates both, this stone helps you when you meditate to reach a little deeper and a little higher to achieve your own best harmonic connection with the Allness.

Atlantisite is a lovely composite cooked up by mother nature with two known materials of Stichtite and Serpentine.

Stichtite is a mineral, a carbonate of chromium and magnesium; formula $Mg6Cr2CO3(OH)16 \cdot 4H2O$.

Serpentine Shown as its name in most stores and the color is usually seen as a pea to hunter (dark forest) green. It has jagged or squiggly lines running through it of lighter and darker material. The more translucent or gem like serpentine has a shiny to waxy appearance $D_2[Si_2O_5](OH)_4$.

The First Position...

... Beginning with when you were first born, people who held you felt an almost instant connection with "I'm all right" and that they have always been loved. I'm sure many people felt you were a very sweet baby.

The Second Position...

… This stone indicates that you were a very deep feeling child and a little on the quiet side. If you made messes it was because you were in the process of creating or making something.

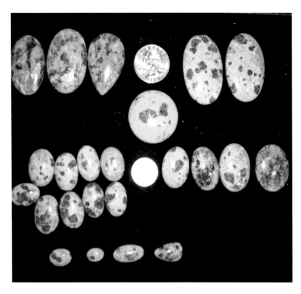

The Third Position...

… You became who you are today through the processes and events of your teenage years. Many of the things that mark who you are today can link back to what occurred during these years. This is where the cocoon of "YOU" happened.

The Fourth Position...

... You needed to let loose of the stories, dramas and significant events that shaped your family. You needed to find your place that you could begin to polish and facets of who you are. This wasn't about disliking or not loving your family and friends as much as it was about creating you from a new place.

The Fifth Position...

… You are in the process of creating a bridge between you and the Allness. Whether you pray, meditate or contemplate. Do so freely with the emphasis connecting with the place your soul is most comfortable, that place of peace for you. This is a gift, receive it in service that it is given to you in. A piece of Danburite might help with this.

The Sixth Position...?

... Freedom is coming to you. To float completely free, you need to release (not sever or cut) the strings that are holding you down... You do not need to burn any bridges... Be committed to floating along the waters in a free state.

Aventurine

...Aventurine adds luster to your own internal spark. It is a stone best described as a charisma magnifier, because it works on your magnetic field, electric, and your aura and helps interconnect them. It helps you become a better communicator and is good for health and vitality. Aventurine is extremely receptive to the form that it occupies. It was used by the ancients to help people shift away from negative personality habits and disruptive physical habits.

The name gives away one of its secrets. A-Ventur is Italian for "a chance" so this is a great stone for gamblers or the venture capitalist. Aventurine is most commonly found in green, but it may also be orange, brown, yellow, blue, or gray. It is also considered to be a great overall health stone and to keep you free from colds and other health annoyances. Aventurine is found in India, Chile, Spain, Russia, Brazil, Austria, and Tanzania. It is a 6.5 on the Mohs scale of hardness. This mineral is sometimes confused with amazonite or jade.

The First Position...

...You must have been one of those giggly, happy babies who made everyone smile when they saw them. Your early years were entertaining and exploratory for you. You may have gotten shocked or burned by playing with something you shouldn't have been. You may even have gotten lost while exploring.

The Second Position...

...This early time was spent exploring or "checking things out." You pushed a lot of buttons and checked out all the edges of the envelope. This may or may not have played out well. You took the energies you were born with and tried to apply them everywhere.

The Third Position...

...You were either popular with the kids your own age or were entertained by watching what others did. You may even have been curious about how you "got away with things" while other people always got caught and were in trouble for. This may even be where you started to enjoy risk because it paid off for you.

The Fourth Position...

...Your leap into the adult world that you are making or made, allowed you to land on your feet, and you made out pretty well no matter what you tried. Even when you found

yourself in a bad situation it was only to "set you up" for something better. If this is you right now, secure this "best situation," if you can, before you are 27 because it won't last forever.

The Fifth Position...

...Go ahead and take that risk or gamble that is on the edge...If you give it your all you will land on your feet in golden shoes...Have that ADVENTURE!

The Sixth Position...?

... Some awesome opportunity is coming your way, and it is going to make you shine...SHINE ON!

Bloodstone

Bloodstone was thought to offer its bearer protection, vitality, and spiritual connection and was worn and carried by knights of the Crusades because the red of the stone symbolized the blood of Christ. It has also been discovered to help speed healing after a surgery or wound. It is excellent to use to enhance the healing of an organ or blood condition. Bloodstone is said to ease difficult menstrual episodes.

Bloodstone is a dark-green variety of the silica mineral Chalcedony that has deposits of bright-red Jasper distributed throughout. Polished sections therefore show red spots on a dark-green background. It shares physical properties with those of quartz. But unlike quartz, its finish and luster can be marred or scratched.

Bloodstone, according to the ancient chart is the birthstone for March.

"A ROMAN BLOODSTONE "MAGIC" GEM

circa 3rd–4th century AD.
One side of the flat oval stone engraved with the anguipede and cock-headed solar deity Abrasax, the cuirassed body frontal, a round shield in his left hand, a whip in his upraised right hand, framed by the letters IAW; the other side with a three line palindromic inscription, BLAN AQANAL BA
1 in. (2.5 cm) high"
Copied from www.christiesinternational.com

All kinds of powers have been ascribed to bloodstone, and it was worn by priests, Kings, and warriors. Ancient Mystics believed bloodstone gave off audible sounds as a guide or for insight. It gives one the ability to banish evil and negativity of all kinds.

Bloodstone can be found in Australia, Brazil, China, India, the Kathiawar Peninsula and the US (Wyoming).

A large bloodstone statue or piece would be excellent for a healing center, doctor's or chiropractor's office, sports medicine clinic or martial arts training school. It is not a good idea to combine Bloodstone with Rose Quartz, Pink Calcite, or Ruby because it can be adverse in some situations.

The First Position...

...You were probably a somber or quiet baby: this doesn't mean sad or depressed. In fact, you may have been considered a very "good" baby because of how quiet you were. You used this time to adjust onto your path as a warrior, healer, or priest.

The Second Position...

...You probably found it very easy to be spiritual as a small child because of your feelings of constant connection. You found it easy to offer verbal help or advice to kids at school and at home...People may have been amazed at your advanced wisdom.

The Third Position...

...If you rebelled at all it was due to the unfairness you saw other people endure. You had a strong connection to your own internal compass or sense of conscious, with the result that people may have looked at you as "odd," yet that didn't affect your self-image because you knew you were operating "rightly." It bothered you to see other people "picked on." You may even have challenged other people's erroneous thinking and offered them the truth... which wasn't always well-received.

The Fourth Position...

... Bloodstone indicates that you launched into your adult years with the idea of doing things the RIGHT way—setting your path on the right track. This period was or is full of lessons for you about learning the difference between "right" and "right for you." This period may give you (or may have given you) the opportunity to dabble and/or prepare for your role as a warrior, a healer, or a priest.

The Fifth Position...

...This period for you is either about learning the lessons of a warrior, healer, or priest that you didn't learn earlier. Learning for the first time that the greatest lesson is to have all of that skill and not be allowed to use it to help or defend something and/or someone you care about. Because it or they won't let you.

So, this is about you getting to know the real reason you are here...your calling. Look again at the stone in position one and see how you might re-integrate those energies and become that person again. You do not have to learn this the hard way...you can also learn through service.

The Sixth Position...?

...Get a check up with a full set of blood tests—if the doctors say you are "fine," then simply clean up your nutritional habits and get on at least a good multi-vitamin with iron. If you have already done this, I would go to the five or six people you are closest to and ask them what is going on with them with no expectation that they will follow your advice because your next lesson is the greatest lesson: to have all the necessary resources and skills and not being allowed to use them to help or defend something and/or someone you care about because it or they won't let you.

<u>Calcite</u>

Calcite comes in the whole rainbow of colors that starts at clear and goes to black. Sometimes it's completely cloudy or muddy and sometimes it is clear enough to see through, like glass. It isn't used in rings because of its softness and not too many people wear them as beads, but you can find it in pendants and carvings.

The largest documented single crystals of calcite originated from Iceland, measured 7×7×2 m and 6×6×3 m and weighed about 250 tons, but there are many pieces that will fit into your pocket and your life. If you feel your piece needs to be cleared, do not treat it like a crystal —if you do, you may end up with some salty-colored water. Use a piece of black Kyanite to pull out any negativity or adverse energy.

Here's Wikipedia's description. "Calcite <u>crystals </u>are <u>trigonal-rhombohedral</u>, though actual calcite <u>rhombohedra </u>are rare as natural crystals. However, they show a remarkable variety of habits including acute to obtuse rhombohedra, tabular forms, <u>prisms</u>, or various <u>scalenohedra</u>. Calcite exhibits several <u>twinning </u>types adding to the variety of observed forms. It may occur as fibrous, granular, lamellar, or compact. Cleavage is usually in three directions parallel to the rhombohedron form. Its fracture is conchoidal, but difficult to obtain. It has a <u>Mohs hardness </u>of 3, a <u>specific gravity </u>of 2.71, and its luster is vitreous in crystallized varieties. Color is white or none, though shades of gray, red, yellow, green, blue, violet, brown, or even black can occur when the mineral is charged with impurities." (http://en.wikipedia.org/wiki/Calcite)

That's the science—now let's dabble in the back story and metaphysics. Vast Calcite seas existed over 400 million years ago; since then, the earth's plates have moved and moved again and this is one of the reasons it can be found in every continent and country in the world. Calcite can be used in combination with itself or other stones, crystals, or gems for the purposes of a talisman or as a healing tool.

The ancient Vedics and Gurus of India taught that really clear Calcite can help you see into other dimensions—if you use it to read a newspaper, you will download more insight into what is "going on." Also called Iceland Spar, **Optical Calcite** works to clear and activate all of the chakras, improving the flow of energy throughout the subtle bodies. Meditation with Optical Calcite can help to improve one's perception of the physical world and of the self, creating a shift in those who experience predominantly negative emotions.

Angel Wing Calcite is an incredible crystal from Mexico. Aligned with the Crown Chakra, Angel Wing Calcite is beneficial when communicating with higher powers. It helps to release disharmony and negative energy from the body. Angel Wing Calcite improves one's perceptions, helping one to see things in a new way. It helps one to shine celestial light on a problem in order to get to the root of it.

Blue Calcite promotes positive abundance and enhances clarity of thought and communication. It embodies the Light of Spirit and spiritual strength. Blue Calcite helps young children with the grieving process and works well during family counseling. This form of Calcite would be great for a family counseling center, but would require cleansing with black Kyanite after every use or daily.

Honey Calcite is light in color like bee pollen and works in clearing the immune system. It affects your body, mind, and Spirit with an energetic warmth, like the first rays of sunlight to shine on you after a very long, cold stretch of winter. It's great for working with the fifth meridian on sexual issues.

Green calcite is a gentle source of health and vitality. It dispels negativity and cleanses the heart chakra. Green Calcite draws abundance and is excellent for releasing issues relating to money or to help someone clear self-worth issues. While the Irish mines were hoarded by the English for their gold and silver, the Irish thought Green Calcite to be a part of a Leprechaun's skeleton and that the "bones" were lucky.

Pink Calcite vibrates to the essence of all possibilities within the self. It touches the Divine Child in the depths of our being, reminding us of pure innocence and primordial bliss. It assists one in manifesting trust and gentleness. It contains all seven rays of the rainbow spectrum and facilitates rebirth into the new age. It is an excellent stone for comfort, peace, and manifesting all possibilities.

Orange Calcite is considered the Vitamin C of the mineral world; this stone is excellent for vitality. Working in the Second Chakra, Orange Calcite helps the body to absorb solar energy. It also helps to sustain faith by working with the mind and spirit....

For the purpose of the Ancient Stone Reading, I will use the four most common and readily available forms of calcite (pink, orange, green and blue).

Blue Calcite

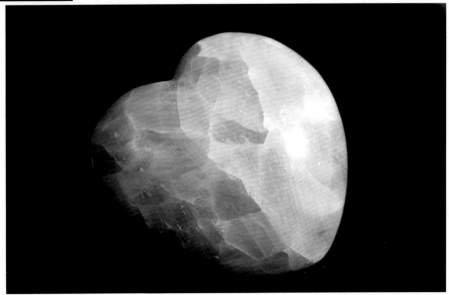

Blue Calcite promotes positive abundance and enhances clarity of thought and communication. It embodies the Light of Spirit and spiritual strength. Blue Calcite helps young children with the grieving process and works well during family counseling. This form of calcite would be great for a family counseling center, but would require cleansing with black kyanite after every use or daily.

The First Position...
...You were a gift to those around you in the family you were born into. As you grew and blossomed it was the gift you gave rather than what you got. The role you fulfilled was essential.

The Second Position...
...Even as a young child you saw through to the truth and felt a source of inner light; while some may not have appreciated the deep insight you had, others marveled at the wisdom beyond your years. Strength and resolve were your companions.

The Third Position...
...You were a counselor to your friends and sometimes the foolish adults around you. Cutting through to the truth is an awesome tool for good, but it can also be an exceptionally destructive one. Letting the truth unfold naturally is not a weakness—it is patience.

The Fourth Position...

...You are gifted with a unique insight and marvel at what others do not see as plainly as you do. You found or find what you are looking for fairly quickly (be careful what you ask for and exactly how you ask for it).

The Fifth Position...

...You are now or are becoming very comfortable with what you believe. You have accumulated experiences that now help you to know that you are correct. Be cautious of self-righteousness.

The Sixth Position...?

...Regrets are coming to a close. You are on the path to receive positive abundance, clarity of thought and spiritual strength.

Green Calcite

Green calcite is a gentle source of health and vitality. It dispels negativity and cleanses the heart chakra. Green Calcite draws abundance and is excellent for releasing issues relating to money or to help someone clear self-worth issues. While the Irish mines were hoarded by the English for their gold and silver, the Irish thought Green Calcite to be a part of a Leprechaun's skeleton and that the "bones" were lucky.

The First Position...
... People simply felt good while they held you, and couldn't seem to wipe the smile off their face for the whole day. Even your close friendships and relationships today feel better when you are around.

The Second Position...
… As a young child you had a hard time dealing with a feeling of negativity around your home—you may even have cried if people were upset.

The Third Position...
…You had a hard time dealing with confrontation as a teen and even if you can handle it now, the "having to handle it" upsets you in and of itself.

The Fourth Position...
...You jumped off into the world with little or no planning and yet somehow landed on your feet while leaving your childhood behind to become a young adult. Many have accused you of BEING lucky.

The Fifth Position...
… Now is the perfect time to get out of your own way. Put aside your thoughts or doubts about your ability to be rewarded. The universe is trying to reward you—open the door and get out of your own way.

The Sixth Position...?
..Your efforts are going to pay off soon or are paying off already.

Orange Calcite

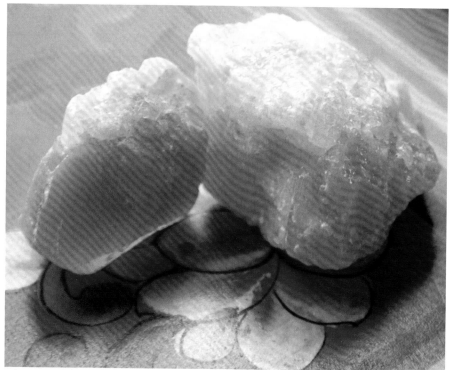

Orange Calcite is considered the Vitamin C of the mineral world; this stone is excellent for vitality. Working in the Second Chakra, Orange Calcite helps the body to absorb solar energy. It also helps to sustain faith by working with the mind and spirit.

The First Position...

...You came into this life and spent your early years with a lot pop and fizzle. You were an adjustment for most people and then they began to crave having you around.

The Second Position...

...You were very vibrant as a young child; this was very taxing on some people, but others just loved the way you could play all day long. Nap times were a serious challenge but you were always better after a rest.

The Third Position...

...You didn't just take someone's word for it because they were older or because it was written down in a book. Life needed to be proven, not just accepted by you. If you were not "rebellious" you were at least trying at times. Remember to get your rest.

The Fourth Position...

...Proving your worth to the world at large is definitely part of your reason for venturing out into the world. This isn't to say you have left home physically, because you still like the comforts of home after you go out to confront or "prove" your importance to the world. It's okay to take an educated risk, but remember to get your rest.

The Fifth Position...

…Let Go. Step out in faith. Quit playing it safe...venture into the water a bit more and let go of the rope. Nothing is going to eat you and you won't die. Venture or be satisfied with nothing.

The Sixth Position...?

...You are about to get a big dose of life-giving force if you will be open to it. Whatever your question, interest or fantasy was that brought you to a desire to have a reading today...it is about to (or has) shown up. Accept it and embrace it. Vitality, health, love, romance, opportunity or prosperity is yours BUT you have to open up to it!

Pink Calcite

Pink Calcite vibrates to the essence of all possibilities within the self. It touches the Divine Child in the depths of our being, reminding us of pure innocence and primordial bliss. It assists one in manifesting trust and gentleness. It contains all seven rays of the rainbow spectrum and facilitates rebirth into the new age. It is an excellent stone for comfort, peace, and manifesting all possibilities.

The First Position...

... All children are special and being around any baby puts a smile on most people's faces. I have held babies that, when they looked up at you, you could feel the smile coming from your toes or deep inside of you. The Pink Calcite in this position indicates that you came in as such a child. A radiator and reminder of the divine sweetness that is there for all of us (we just lose connection to it).

The Second Position...

…The Pink Calcite child is a hopeless optimist and is always finding the good in everything. This is something for the parents or guardians around them to be watchful for with other adults. These children also have a very active imagination.

The Third Position...

…Your teenage years were the creating, drafting, and molding of your giving personality. You were the one always willing to help...Be cautious about this tendency. Allow **yourself** to grow, instead of only helping everyone else to grow. Do not use the excuse that you were so busy helping someone that you didn't do what you were supposed to do....Remember, your accomplishments can feed you too.

The Fourth Position...

...Whether at work or at home, you are everyone's helper. Don't block other people's growth by preventing them from answering for their actions or by doing too much for them. If you made a list of everything you needed to do...how many of those items would be assisting others? Find value in who you are, not just what you bring to others.

The Fifth Position...

...Emotionally and spiritually you are or will soon be at the end of the rainbow, reaping a reward that is overflowing.

The Sixth Position...?

... Comfort, peace, and manifesting all possibilities is just around the corner for you.

Carnelian (Agate)

Carnelian is full of life, passion, and force. It allows living to the fullest and that the bearer speaks boldly in this world or in the others. It breaks up negativity in the bearer of this stone and helps the facilitator to move those who are addicted into more positive behaviors. Like the goddess Pele, Carnelian is the fire of life and the passion for it.

Agates in general are best regarded as "A GATE." They are portals, openings, doorways, or hallways that lead to other spaces you are not currently in. Depending on the position of the Agate in the reading and/or the question being asked, it can also mean that you need to find a portal, opening, doorway, or hallway. Agates are especially useful in opening chakra and meridians on the body during stone layouts for healing purposes.

"Carnelian (also spelled cornelian) is a reddish-brown mineral which is commonly used as a semi-precious gemstone. Similar to carnelian is sard, which is generally harder and darker. (The difference is not rigidly defined, and the two names are often used interchangeably.) Both carnelian and sard are varieties of the silica mineral chalcedony colored by impurities of iron oxide. The color can vary greatly, ranging from pale orange to an intense almost-black coloration."
(http://en.wikipedia.org/wiki/Carnelian~~from Wikipedia~~)

Carnelian has been found in archaeological digs on crowns, jeweled thrones, and other furniture dating back to pre-Egyptian times. It is an ancient radiator of regal power and authority. It would be difficult to find it absent from any royal family's jewelry to this day. It was used by ancient tribal leaders as the topmost stone on their weapon or staff. Carnelian is a 7 on the Mohs scale and has been used for centuries to carve beautiful cameos. Dignitaries and other members of authority would wear it as a buckle, or as an accent on a broach or pendant. It is found in Australia, Brazil, Madagascar, Russia, South Africa and the US.

Energetically, it burns through resistance and can help you discover areas or items in your life that need to be removed or burned away so that you can move forward. This isn't a scary stone. Farmer's fields have to occasionally be burned before they can be replanted. Fire has been used forever to cook and heat. Volcanoes build anew after the eruption.   When passions cool, Carnelian helps to re-fire them, and I'm not speaking of just sex. Passion for life, work, experience, travel, education, or love are all equally important.

Generally when something cools or you become dispassionate about any area of life that used to "fire you up," it's because someone or some thing has created a block in that area...Allow Carnelian to help burn it away.

Carnelian is listed in the ancient Arabic, Hebrew, Italian and Roman tables as a Zodiac birthstone for the signs of Leo and Virgo. Folklore suggests that carnelian was used to protect the traveler, after death and to guard against evil.

Carnelian's healing properties are thought to help purify the blood and relieve menstrual cramps and back pain. It is also thought to be beneficial in the treatment of infertility and is worn to enhance passion and desire.

The First Position...

...You were a very active, driven child...full of life and always about discovery...maybe you even have a few physical scars to show for it.

The Second Position... A lot of things must have melted away in your early
childhood—you may not even remember much of it. Being "safe or secure" may be difficult for you, but that hasn't diminished your ability to want to be engaged in whatever experience there may be for you.

The Third Position...

Carnelian here means you were challenging many things openly...being accused of being rebellious was part of it. However, you were not as much rebellious as you just required proof of things. You didn't just accept or believe things just because others thought you should.

The Fourth Position.

You launched or you are about to launch out away from your childhood like a rocket taking off. Everything that you are not intending to keep will burn away. OR, what the universe feels is best that you let lose of will also burn away. Be very mindful that you can simple release it into the flame, or it can be burnt away while you tightly hold onto it. There is a lot of good that will come from this ash.

The Fifth Position... You are now or you will be the phoenix—you have already lost

(or burned) all that you need to...Spread your wings and catch the winds of plenty that are flowing your way.

The Sixth Position...

If you haven't been going through a series of losses, now is the time to remind yourself to let things go easily, knowing that if they are meant to be yours they will return. The tighter you try to hold on, the more difficult an experience you will have. Eventually, you will pass through this experience and then your life will begin to grow with vigor and vitality. This isn't a protracted (long) experience unless you make it so. If you light a piece of string with flame it is burnt up and gone in a second....If you encase it in wax it burns for a much longer time...If you then insist on holding the candle in your hand while it burns, it is painful and long-lasting. So, release and pass through this experience to become the phoenix soaring on wings of reward

CELESTITE

Celestite contains the essence of celestial realms, accessing higher dimensions of reality and is excellent for astral travel and lucid dream states. Attunes artistry to higher realms and creates profound peace, beauty and clarity.

Used by my ancestors to help or heal those with bone weakness or disorders. It was used to treat someone that suffered from pessimism. Used as part of a cure (combined with danburite) to heal someone suffering from a spiritual illness. Was used to stop nightmares as well.

The largest known geode is 35 feet long and you can stand up in it. It's on South Bass Island on Lake Erie, near Put-In-Bay Ohio.

Celestite is a strontium sulfate mineral that sometimes contains calcium or barium. Can be found to be colorless or pink, pale green, pale brown, black and (most commonly) light or pale blue.

The First Position...

... You were one of those angelic babies that made everyone smile when they see you. I'm sure that everyone wanted to hold you as well. When people held you they felt supported and nurtured, which is mostly how the people that are close to you feel when they are around you now.

The Second Position...

... The world came to you as a bit of a surprise. You may have even hid behind the friendly leg of your mom and dad, not because you were afraid... it was just so you could get a good look at the situation first before you engaged... It has been a long time since you were "surprised", but you still approach life with an air of caution. There is an old saying that fools rush in where angels fear to tread... You are not a fool and you MAY be an angel.

The Third Position...

... You may not have been a leader when you we a teenager, but you were one of the few that didn't often fall for peer pressure. You were a watcher or observer and to this day you do not FALL for things they way others do.

The Fourth Position...

...You went out to find your highest level, to seek a vantage point that you could find to view, where YOU needed to go. Not a point of achievement but, what target to shoot for. Leaving your old world behind was more about finding a direction for your life and not about leaving what was behind you.

The Fifth Position...

... You, down deep in your soul, are in a place of understanding, that you get it. Not an arrogance but, because you know what you know it is a place of peace and grace. That only knowing yourself and your place in the universe can bring. You can ACT any way that you wish... the difference is you know when you are acting up, or out, for someone's benefit.

The Sixth Position...?

... You are going to find out (may already have a clue) what is still here for you. Of course, there are those that still need you but I'm speaking of finding a better course for you. A piece of carnelian might help you burn away the fog, so you can see it more clearly.

CHRYSOCOLLA

It assists in grounding and stabilizing the energies of the chakras and merridians. Can initiate powerful visionary experiences through the third eye. This stone has a deep connection with Mother Earth and increases communication, abundance and Life Force.

It assists in promoting inner physical strength. It helps purify the body, home and environment. The name was used by Theophrastus (315 B.C.) and comes from the Greek chrysos, meaning "gold," and kolla, meaning "glue," the name of the material used to solder gold.

Formula: $Cu_{2-x}Al_x(H_{2-x}Si_2O_5)(OH)_4 \cdot nH_2O$

Luster: Earthy

Hardness: 2½ – 3½

The First Position...

... Dreams, goals and plans were generated by your arrival; dreams and goals for you thought up by your parents. Goals and thoughts of the future were inspired by you with everyone that held you.

The Second Position...

… You were probably a very curious toddler. Some people would have interpreted your energy as wanting to discover while others wondered why you were always getting into things.

The Third Position...

… You were a great participant of other people's ideas...I hope you used this to help with positive activities rather than following down an ill path. Did you cave into teen pressure or use this trait on committees in high school?

The Fourth Position......

When you left your childhood behind, it was to find your own healthy environment and a place that you could grow. To begin anew. This was a time of dreams and ambitions for you. Similar dreams may yet be able to be accomplished as long as you are willing to share the credit and the vision.

The Fifth Position...

Your environment seems to have gotten a yucky, sticky substance coating it. If you haven't recently done this, you need to clean up your emotional, mental, physical and spiritual environments... Do a cleaning of your home, your mind, a cleanse of the body and spiritual renewal... something icky got stuck and needs to be removed.

The Sixth Position...?

... you are coming into a time of renewal and a relighting of your hidden fire. Welcome and accept it as a good thing. Maybe you will take up a creative art (or get reacquainted with and older endeavor). Let this time of vitality spring into you like the warm rays of sunshine after a long winter.

Citrine

This yellow, brown, or golden variety of Quartz is one of only two stone or mineral varieties on our planet that don't hold negative energy, rather dissipating and/or transmuting it.

Citrine helps its bearer to accumulate wealth and material abundance maybe due to its ability to increase mental focus and endurance.

If worn as a ring or a pendant, it cleans and clears the aura while aligning the aura with the physical body. In order to accomplish this, it re-boots or restores the body's electrical system. Increased creativity and enhanced visioning have also been some of the reported effects.

The First Position...

...You came into this life to help others move forward by either leading them towards the next event or learning opportunity or participating in the same. The more you move in this direction, the closer you move toward making your own dreams become a reality.

The Second Position...

...In becoming aware of the world around you, you were able to keep the negativity from sticking to you. There were many dramas in the life of others yet you were able to disassociate yourself from other people's games.

The Third Position...

...You began to sense a "MORE" side to life. You may have begun to sense, see, or feel the auras of electrical fields around others and objects in general and/or sensing or seeing gave you a better insight into situations and complexities.

The Fourth Position...

...You make things happen. Things get done through you or because of you. You inspire or you push. You are a force in the current of life, like a large ship moving across a body of water.

The Fifth Position...

...You are moving toward resolution...not negative not positive, just done. The more you become aware of the forces, currents, flows, and fields around you, the sooner you will achieve 'finished.'

The Sixth Position...?

...You will begin to work with those fields, currents, and flows of energy and substance to create sustainable resource reality for yourself. Awaken yourself to releasing all the negativity and/or blockages in your life and your vision...or do not and have not.

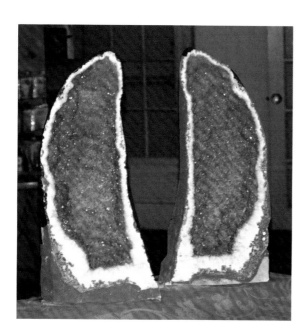

DANBURITE

This stone has a color range from colorless to yellow to pink and white. It simulates the third eye and crown chakras. They carry a very high vibration which allows one to access inner guidance, attain higher states and increase communication with the Angelic realm. Without Hope, the people perish"... Lack of faith can be fatal.

Can be found Almost everywhere except South America,, Most of what we carry comes from Mexico. Health wise it is good for your bones and teeth. Holding Danburite Just makes You FEEL BETTER.
Formula: $CaB_2Si_2O_8$
Color:Pale yellow,
.Luster:Vitreous, Greasy
Hardness:7 – 7½

The name came from where it was first discovered, in modern times,. Danbury Conneticut.

The First Position...

... As a baby, people felt connected to the love of the universe simply by holding you for the first time. You have always been able to tap this inner strength whenever you have felt like you needed to "keep going". Others still draw upon this strength as well, but you need to not let them drain you completely.

The Second Position...

... You may have had a hard time learning to relate to a world that had so little love in it. As a toddler you also had a kind of Divine light that lit up a room when you entered. During your grade school years you may have had other children pick on you or act out in your direction so they could "brush up" against the light you shared.

The Third Position...

... You were a comfort to many people in your teenage years, Being an angel without the wings can be an adjustment. This isn't to say that you were always "good", but you always had good motives.

\

The Fourth Position...

... You left your childhood behind and moved into adulthood with the desire to find your own guidance. If that came from an external or internal source was fine as long as it was yours and not dictated to you by another.

The Fifth Position...

... An awareness of "everything is going to be all right" is dawning or will dawn on the horizon of your consciousness. Things are beginning to fit and you can see or feel their alignment.

The Sixth Position...?

... Your life is moving into a good place. The worries you have had will resolve and/or you will be at peace with where they are. Your connection to all that is, will feel like it is a part of you.

Fairy Cross

Chiastolite and Andalusite are both scientific names For Fairy Cross. It has an optical phenomenon in which mineral grains within the rock appear to be different colors when observed at different angles. The aluminum silica structure allows the bearer to have an additional alertness to the world around them by hyper-activating the sensory centers of the brain. Excellent for horses and humans because it positively bridges (or crosses) the emotional, spiritual and physical aspects.

The First Position...

... You brought sweetness to the world around you because the energy you brought in with you was love. Everyone got a charge of the celestial essence whenever they held you as a new baby.

The Second Position...

... It would not be surprising to hear that you had lots of imaginary (meaning ones that other people didn't see) friends when you were little. You definitely saw the world as "MORE than" other people saw it... The good news is you still can.

The Third Position...

... These years were probably very difficult for you as you struggled to make sense out of the path people wanted you to take and the many other paths you saw (or subconsciously perceived) for yourself and others. Hopefully, you were honored for the different way you saw things.

The Fourth Position...

... You tried to bring a lot of your life with you (from your childhood and high school years) into your adult years and found it painful when those areas dropped away. You hopefully learned to live in the now instead of longing for what was or could have been.

The Fifth Position...

… You need to see yourself as being whole and not living separate lives within the one you are living now. You do not need to be a different person at work, home, church or in social settings. You can accomplish this by allowing the bridges and crossing (like what this stone symbolizes) to help you retrieve those things about your past that worked for you. You do not need to live in the past, take back and incorporate those things that helped you to be your best.

The Sixth Position...?

... You are about to boost your perceptions and ability to understand the world and it's "mini" complexities. The almost taken paths, turn arounds and dead ends on your life path have lessons also... Re-examine those to receive your next insights.

Fluorite

Named from the Latin "to flow," Fluorite enhances the flow of energy through the physical, emotional, and spiritual bodies. This stone is excellent for meditation as it calms the mind and opens one to higher levels of awareness. It is a reminder of perfect physical health and optimal mental well-being. A source of calcium fluoride, this stone is excellent for bones, teeth, and blood and protects against colds and flu. Self-discipline, inner strength, spiritual balance, and the ability to light up the dark places within us are all qualities associated with Fluorite.

Fluorite grows or, rather, develops with a cubical style of growth, comes in a wide range of colors (with purple being its most common color), and is found around the planet. Sometimes the color is well-mixed throughout the formation; occasionally the coloration has an internal gradient (or rainbow) and the color also shows up as a crust or attached layer on top of a clearer Fluorite base.

Linguistically, the word is derived from the Latin word *"flou" (meaning to flow).* Science believes this is due to its low melting point; we know its because Fluorite helps your energies to "Flow Right." Science and the mining industry consider Fluorite to be part of a gangue (something that is mixed or an overburden for a commercially viable substance or ore); we know it to be the attractant that brought components together through its frequency that made the "valuable" substance possible. This is why Fluorite is able to keep the flow going as it draws what is valuable to the person possessing it.

Fluorescence is only available with Fluorite, not to be confused with luminescence. When Fluorite is exposed to UV (or blacklight), it (like many other materials) shines in a different coloration than it does under regular light. However, science has not adequately explained why Fluorite is reflectively brighter under blacklight than it is under normal light and other materials are the same or less reflective under UV than they are in standard light. We know the reflectivity is because of Fluorite's ability to "light up" deep hidden issues though its enhanced ability to handle magnetics and frequency that is only illustrated when you put it under black light.

The First Position...

..."All is right with the world" is the way people felt when they held you as a baby. One of the reasons you came in was to help people find their own level of balance or stasis. You may still have a problem when your world is tossing you around or is in chaos.

The Second Position...

...You may have been impatient as a young child because you like to keep things moving. You may have disliked anything that was the same as last week even if it was just finishing left-overs. You were always excited to learn "the next thing."

The Third Position...

...The repetition of life bored you to tears and so public school may have been very difficult for you. You may have been accused of being "easily distracted," but what it really was/is, is that once you have learned it you don't want to spend any more time on it.

The Fourth Position...

...You just have to move on...it's time. That is how you looked at getting away from your family. These years are or were all about experiencing. You can get very "addicted" to things that offer you rapid change of information and experience (like the Internet or digital games) whether they accomplish anything or not. Break away and/or don't get hooked by these kinds of activities. You have too much to offer the world. The flow of life is what you can help others achieve.

The Fifth Position...

...You are now or you are about to embark on a new flow of life. Go with it:, you will enjoy the ride. The experience may challenge your prior notions of how the world works but go with it. This could also indicate that you need to let go of something emotional, intellectual, or spiritual.

The Sixth Position...?

...Being in the flow isn't the same thing as going with the flow. The flow of your life has brought many things to you. You have panned or fished out everything you're going to get from this spot. You get to flow to a new spot. So, cut yourself loose and let the flow begin. A word of caution: make sure you and everyone who is coming with you have cut yourselves loose. If you are standing in a swift-moving river and have a cord tied to both banks, what happens if you only cut one side?

Hematite

Hematite comes in many forms: all have an ability to absorb and radiate laser light equally, which is only one of Hematite's physical miracles. Emotionally it gives what it gets…send love, it sends love back. Mentally this stone is excellent for adding to someone's ability to focus and for helping those who are easily distracted without diminishing their sparkle. Hematite, in its natural form, bonds the energies of different materials: this is why it is excellent at holding and/or bonding with magnetic material. So, it also helps us to join the disassociated parts of ourselves and helps our gifts to rise and sparkle.

Hematite also helps to grow one's charisma without sacrificing integrity to do so. It's a good gift for someone who is beginning a speaking career or sales position. It could be the token stone for actors, ministers, priests, or honest politicians. Because of its ability to provide a spontaneous mirror, it can offer many good lessons for people who are dishonest or those who create unnecessary drama.

My good friend Robert Simmons, in his book entitled *The Book of Stones* that he co-wrote with Naisha, continues to point out that Hematite is an excellent shield for negativity, but that it also reflects back what you create.

Hematite has had many uses in many places because it is harder than the iron it is found with: ancient peoples used it in Rome and Greece as jewelry and seals. It has been called 'black diamond' and has been shaped and used as a black pearl. It was used by Native Americans as spearheads and arrowheads and was thought to make you stronger and harder to hit in battle when ground and worn as war paint.

"Hematite is a mineral colored black to steel or silver-gray, brown to reddish brown, or red. It is <u>mined</u> as the <u>main ore of iron</u>. Varieties include kidney ore, martite (<u>pseudomorphs</u> after <u>magnetite</u>), iron rose, and specularite (specular Hematite). While the forms of Hematite vary, they all have a rust-red streak. Hematite is harder than pure iron, but much more brittle. <u>Maghemite</u> is a Hematite- and <u>magnetite</u>-related oxide mineral.

Huge deposits of Hematite are found in <u>banded iron formations</u>. Grey Hematite is typically found in places where there has been standing water or mineral <u>hot springs</u>, such as those in <u>Yellowstone National Park</u> in the <u>United States</u>. The mineral can <u>precipitate</u> out of water and collect in layers at the bottom of a lake, spring, or other standing water. Hematite can also occur without water, however, usually as the result of <u>volcanic</u> activity.

Clay-sized Hematite crystals can also occur as a secondary mineral formed by weathering processes in soil, and, along with other iron oxides or oxyhydroxides such as Goethite, is responsible for the red color of many tropical, ancient, or otherwise highly weathered soils. Good specimens of Hematite come from England, Mexico, Brazil, Australia, United States, and Canada." (from Wikipedia)   Hematite has been discovered on MARS:

http://www.nasa.gov/vision/universe/solarsystem/release-062504.html

The First Position...

...You were especially sensitive as a baby, so much so that if anyone was upset you got upset—you could be happy and hear another baby crying and then start crying yourself.

The Second Position...

… As a young child you would pick up and repeat anything heard or felt. Other kids liked playing with you because you were "very into" whatever they were into or doing. Unfortunately, this included both good and bad behaviors. And much of the bad stuff you ended up getting blamed for.

The Third Position...

…You have always been a great helper in any project or activity, and I hope you were around "good kids" when you were a teenager. For you it probably didn't feel like pressure (as in "peer pressure"); more like, everybody else was doing it, so why not.

The Fourth Position...

... If you ever left your birth family, you were probably pulled or pushed to do so. Being comfortable is very important to you. You are a team player and if you ever get a "great" team to associate with you will play a championship role with them. You will reflect and amplify those that you associate with.

The Fifth Position...

…You are in a position of reflecting back all the aspects and occurrences of your life. You can choose to mirror those with a great deal of intensity and charisma or you can send out a different energy or impression. To send out something different, spend some time around and/or study people in fact or fiction who reflect the qualities you wish to project.

The Sixth Position...?

...You are or you are about to receive back all that you have sent out in life.

Herkimer Diamond

People who are born under the birthstone of Diamond (under the chart that is 25,000 years old, that is the last month of the year, which is December in our calendar)are strong and firm with sharp minds. The Diamond person doesn't move easily off a position but are staunchly loyal. Diamonds bring longevity, particularly to relationships. Diamonds bring change but, once the change has taken place they offer eventual stasis, clarity and abundance. It can amplify one's thoughts, strengths, and weaknesses. Modern society has popularized this stone but it was not always thought as a loving gift. Always brings change in the bearer.

I like Herkimer diamonds, for the purpose of the readings, because they do not cost as much as their South African counterparts. They come in an awesome array of natural forms but most commonly as the double terminated shape.

In Paul Kessler's book Titled ***MOHAWK - Discovering the Valley of the Crystals Copyright 2002*** I discovered this interesting set of facts *"More important were the clear quartz crystals now called Herkimer diamonds, which could be quarried in a few local mines and abound on Mohawk village sites. These were highly valued by Iroquois and other nations. Kanyenke was more likely "Place of the Crystals." Crystals were symbolically important as amulets of success, health, and long life, artifacts more likely to inspire a name than a second-rate chert. The Mohawks were the main suppliers of quartz crystals up to 1614"*

Scientifically herkimers are listed as quartz, in other words no different from any other quartz. However there are many differences in herkimers and other quartz varieties. One of which is their extreme portions of absolute clarity. They are individually found absolutely clear. So what component in nature cooks impurities out of stone... Carbon. The Herkimer diamond has less carbon than the diamonds in South Africa but, they must be a diamond due to the natural clarity with the carbon element.

Real Diamonds can be used for doing a reading but Herkimers are far less expensive.

The First Position...

... As a baby, changes occurred because of your arrival. You came to remind people of clarity and inspire clear thinking. It maybe easy for you to think in critical terms, not in just a negative sense, but to weigh out what is right and then act on it.

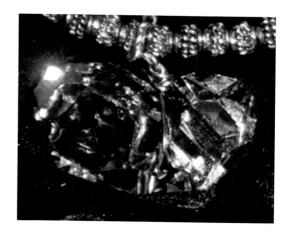

The Second Position...

...There were some major changes that took place for you between the ages of 2 -12 that are still having an effect on how you interpret life now. Examine those and see if you need to keep those same motivations.

The Third Position...

... This is when you developed the skills of helping people through the changes they need to go through. You don't have to keep doing that or you can change it so it benefits you.

The Fourth Position...

... In your late teens or early twenties you will (or are) go through changing everything. You do not need to have negative energy to make change. You can change the way you do things so there is no trail of negativity left behind.

The Fifth Position...

... Life either is now or is about to have some change in it. Please see this for the opportunity that it is. These changes are supposed to be an improvement. Breathe it in and let the universe bless you with what is coming, Let the changes that are coming anyway be a discovery on the trip of life rather than a stumbling block.

The Sixth Position...?

... Change is upon you, do your best to ride it out. All 12 areas of your life are going to shift to accommodate these changes.

Jade

Jade has always been associated with prosperity and wealth. It both represents and attracts accumulation. As you are in the process of attracting wealth and prosperity, be cautious of finding value in every scrap of paper and any substance that passes your way, or you will find yourself buried in what you accumulate.

Jade is a compact, opaque gemstone ranging in color from dark green to almost white. The term is applied to specimens cut from the minerals jadeite and nephrite.

Jadeite, the less common and more highly prized of the two minerals, is a silicate of sodium and aluminum, **$NaAl(SiO_3)_2$,** usually containing some iron, calcium, and magnesium. It belongs to the group of minerals called pyroxenes. Jadeite crystallizes in the monoclinic system but rarely occurs in distinct crystals and is usually found in fibrous, compact, massive aggregates. The luster on a fresh fracture is dull and wax-like, but polished jadeite has a vitreous luster. Nephrite, a member of the amphibole group of minerals, is a silicate of calcium and magnesium, with a small amount of iron replacing part of the magnesium. It is a tough, compact variety of the mineral tremolite. Polished nephrite has an oily luster. Their family name **pyroxenes** means "fire-strangers" because they were first thought to be the result of impurities forming within the soup of volcanic glass but, they were crystals that were there before the volcano erupted and therefore got heat treated by nature to hold their form and coloration. Peridot is also in this family.

The healing power of Jade helps your body to build or rebuild itself. The essential elements of sodium, aluminum, silica, iron, calcium, and magnesium have an effect on your emotional, spiritual, and mental bodies, in that it makes you aware enough to evaluate everything's potential. It's a fire dragon elementally, so if something isn't working or if you haven't considered carefully what you have built, it may give you the opportunity of starting over from scratch.

The First Position...

... You were highly valued when you first showed up on the scene as a baby, and you still offer to your nearest friends and intimate relationships a reminder of their worth and why they keep coming back around to receive more VALUE from you.

The Second Position...

… Your childhood provided others with a series of (hopefully wonderful) surprises of discoveries by you and the little wisdoms that you shared.

The Third Position...

… You were probably a thoughtful teenager and maybe came across as shy to many since you were more contemplative than other kids your age.

The Fourth Position...

... You couldn't wait to get out of your teenage or school years to start adding value to your life. You may have even started working earlier than most ...like during high school. Did you rush too much and miss out on a few things?

The Fifth Position...

… If you will let your body, mind, and spirit do so, you will begin to rebuild your world. Some things will either drift away (if you let them) or burn away (if you try to hold on too tightly).

The Sixth Position...?

...The rewards of what you have built are coming soon. Think about what you have built and the foundation of what you have built on. Do you have the right to expect Mean Dragons or Angels bringing blessings?

Jasper

Jasper has confused me beginning from the time when I first discovered it many years ago, and it has confused many others since it first showed up in the course of human activities many thousands of years ago. Jaspers are silica based, but so is our planet. It can be found black to white and any coloration in between (sometimes all in the same stone). I have crushed Jasper in my hand, and yet some of it is as hard as Quartz crystal. I think we need to come up with a number of new categories or, at least, subcategories to define these wide-ranging, diverse materials from all over the world.

Jaspers are referenced in the Christian Bible and every other religious text on the planet. It was used as a sharpened tool over 5,000 years ago and may have been used by cave men as a spearhead or as a skinning knife.

For an opaque rock, it sure is pretty when it is all polished up. The patterns are created by the "cooking" of minerals while in a molten state. Patterns emerge during the settlement, followed by cracking then resettling, a process that happens over millions of years.

Some types of Jasper have two or three common names for every locale they are found in. Since Jasper is found all over the world...you can begin to see the problem. Geology and science have a hard time with exact classification especially because science likes to classify by both structure and substance. All those beautiful colors and patterns that make Jasper so sought after are also a part of the confusion. It is the substance (minerals and other components) that makes it hard to classify.

Landscape Jasper.... is an awesome swirl of color in softer pastels than we are used to by mother nature. Energetically... it offers smooth waves of energy, good for relaxing or sleep. Therapeutically...Useful in penetrating deep issues or getting through hard (or fortified) emotional walls.

Many jewelry artists use Jasper as a support or foundation stone because it comes from the rudimentary elements we all require. It has been this way for a very long time. In the museums of art and history you can see ancient Gods and Goddesses carved out of many forms of Jasper. The ancient jewelry that adorned both prince and commoner had Jasper as a backing for many of the pieces. Within the context of the *Ancient Stone Reading* book, I will include only Red and Yellow Jasper. I could, and may someday, do an entire book on Jasper—however, these types are among the most common.

Red Jasper

Red Jasper is grounding, works well with the Root Chakra, and enhances strength, is good for blood purification and its protection, and for disorders of the stomach and the liver. Red Jasper is a dense, opaque, micro-crystalline variety of Quartz, usually red or brown with spots of white or yellow and colored by oxides of iron. It is often used as a decorative stone.

The First Position...

... As a baby, you were as special as all other children were and are. You were born with a quiet strength that often times goes unappreciated but is very important to the continuation of our human lives.

The Second Position...

... You were not given to flights of fancy, although I'm sure you enjoyed Disneyland or a cartoon as much as any other kid would. But someone has to be the steady one and it is you.

The Third Position...

... Because of your strength and vital energy you may have been attracted to sports and/or shop class, arts, or crafts. Because you are aptly gifted with your hands, you were or would probably be good at those pursuits throughout your life.

The Fourth Position...

... You left home when it was the right thing for you to do. You are good at putting lives and things together, you probably had a friend (that was a mess) willing to have you for a roommate. You are the type of person who would do really well as a chef or contractor or any other position that requires taking somebody else's design or drawing and making it work.

The Fifth Position...

... Pay attention to the physical working side of your life. It might be a good idea to get your home's electrical and plumbing checked and maybe yours, too. Take some time to check out all the functional and practical aspects of your life. Taking a good vitamin supplement couldn't hurt either.

The Sixth Position...?

... Your life is going to continue to move on as it has in the past. Are you looking for change? If you are willing to pay the price for the change, go for it and draw another stone to see what happens.

Yellow Jasper

Meekness is not weakness—this Jasper enforces your will without inflaming your anger: Gandhi was meek but was far from weak. In fact, this would be an excellent choice for someone trying to get control of rampant emotions. Teenagers who fall into "drama" or "act out" could be well served by carrying a piece of this in their pocket or as a piece of jewelry.

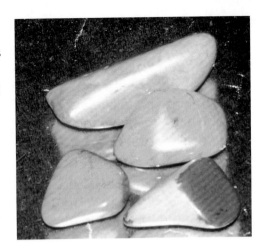

The First Position...

...You are what most Moms would consider a good baby. You probably started sleeping through the night pretty early. Although you were easy to entertain you didn't like to be pulled away from something that fascinated you.

The Second Position...

... Although no one would have called you a bad or willful child, you could definitely let people know if you were dissatisfied. You are the type of child it would have been easy to indulge because you were so easy to be around.

The Third Position...

... As a teenager you may have been the leader of a club or your clique. Maybe you were smarter than everyone else. Be careful not to become a manipulator... become a diplomat instead.

The Fourth Position...

... If you made the break from your family, you have to be careful not to be pulled back into all the things they NEED of you. You can be a strong force in your family and the rest of the world if you let your gentle strength arise.

The Fifth Position...

... You have been a source of strength for those around you. Find your replacement and don't fear it. Your friends and family will always look to you.... but someone else is nearby that can be that soft power source you have always been.

The Sixth Position...?

... Stand fast in your strength. You do not need to "blow up" or show anger. Just disallow other people's bad behavior.

KYANITE

Kyanite This fibrous stone aligns all chakras. Often used in meditation, Kyanite bridges the gap between yourself and your higher self. This is one of two stones that does not absorb negativity.(The other is Citrine). Black Kyanite has strong grounding properties and cleans the lower chakras. This is the one stone that does not absorb negativity but rather dissipate it.

Everything and Everyone has energy. You can judge this to be good or bad but that is a determination or recognition on your part. However there are errant energies that people and things create and emanate. The additional benefit of have a piece of Kyanite in your bag of stones is that it cleans the all the stones in your bag and doesn't then require further cleaning like citrine.

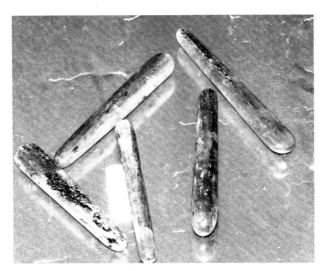

The physical properties are wide and varied. Even its luster varies; vitreous, greasy and pearly, Can be transparent, translucent and opaque. Colors range from blue, black, white, gray, but can occasionally be found in green, yellow, orange and pink. It is always brittle when you break it, but can break cleanly to fibrous (or splintery). Even the hardness ranges with a wide gap of 5-7. Kyanite specimens can be found from the polar ice caps and everywhere in between, with the very best specimens, usually, coming from Afghanistan. Al_2SiO_5 is it's exact formula with it's primary elements being Aluminum, Silica and Oxygen. It is not radioactive, but that doesn't mean it can't handle energies. It was first used in spark plugs and refractories. Works well with magnetism and regulates the energy of frequencies.

It works well with all the bodies' energies: spiritual, mental and emotion while driving away the errant energy of other people.

The First Position...

... As a baby you helped people to get a taste of what it felt like to be in alignment with the higher aspects of their lives.

The Second Position...

... In your early family life you helped them to shift from negative behaviors, you could have been important for your parents staying together or your siblings becoming closer or your whole family becoming more of one.

The Third Position...

... People would want to put things on you (blame, their responsibilities or their power), even if this stuck to you externally in some way, it didn't shape you the way it did others. You rarely take on other peoples stuff... that doesn't mean you don't care, you just don't make their problems yours.

The Fourth Position...

... You were tired of the drama you grew up in and HAD to get away from it. You needed to cut a different path away from all the stuff around your childhood.

The Fifth Position...

... Other peoples stuff is dragging you down and the universe agrees. You have to get away from it. Your emotional and spiritual bodies are being assaulted by how deeply you get involved to "help" other people. Time to get away from it so you can heal.

The Sixth Position...?

... You need to let loose of your judgments. You have a eternal criteria that people have to live up to, You have judgments that you have passed onto society. You need to let all that go and it begins with your judgment of you. You can accomplish this by taking a moment at the beginning of each day to center and tell yourself to release... maybe even ask the universe to help. OR you can wait until it is ripped from you in some less than pleasant fashion.

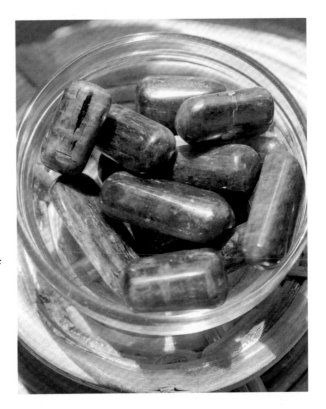

Labradorite

Labradorite is called the Magic Stone. Using it, a sudden change of circumstances will bring you what you want—thus, the old adage: be very careful what you wish for as you may just get it. Labradorite is a form of feldspar. This stone mirrors the deep wisdom of the unconscious. It represents the layers of dimensional and earth energies.

Labradorite is an excellent tool for shape shifting and shamanic journeying through time and other worlds. It represents the Raven of American Indian medicine acting as a messenger from other realms. It is a token stone of the Squirrel in the Tree of Life traditions because of the way it allows the user to cross dimensions. The way it helps to bring magic and miracles and its ability to help its user to scry has also branded it as "the Merlin Stone." Attunement to one's path of destiny has made Labradorite a very popular jewelry material with its subtle blue, red, or yellow lustrous range. Its subtle shifts can almost be missed on the bigger pieces unless turned into the light.

The First Position...

... Your mother's pregnancy with you may have been a surprise but not as surprising as you have been. As a little child, you may have surprised people by the things you could do or where they would have found you.

The Second Position...

… You were probably very good at "hide and seek" as a child or helping people to find their keys or other things they had misplaced. You were also good at bringing out the hidden layers in people.

The Third Position...

... OOOooo! You could have been very interesting to know if you wanted to be ... not nice. You had or you have a way of getting under people's skin to either encourage or annoy them. The gift reflected by Labradorite will always help you find what is hidden.

The Fourth Position...

... You pulled away from your birth family by deciding what and where your differences were. Be careful about continuing this behavior in other relationships because you had or you have a way of getting under people's skin to either encourage or annoy them. The gift reflected by Labradorite will always help you find what is hidden, but be careful how you use it.

The Fifth Position...

... Truth is coming and so will healing, but not at the same time. You may have even begun to put some of the pieces together or at least received the raw facts.

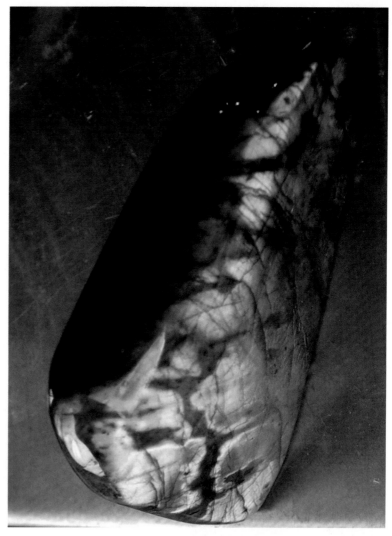

However don't JUMP to a conclusion until you are sure you have all the information. Healing will begin after the layer(s) of truth are before you. This stone mirrors the deep wisdom of the unconscious. It represents the layers of dimensional and earth energies.

The Six Position...?

... Labradorite is called the Magic Stone. A sudden change of circumstances will bring you what you want. Be very careful what you wish for and be mindful of the way you ask, as you may just get it. Think of your life in a more conscious fashion. Make a plan and wish it forward.

Lapis Lazuli

This deep blue stone has been referred to as the "stone of total awareness," providing for the activation of the throat and brow chakras and allowing for conscious attunement to the intuitive and psychic aspects of being. It can also assist one in gaining access to esoteric planetary knowledge and hidden sacred texts. It may also be used to gain personal insight into dreams. Lapis lazuli is an ancient gem, and as such, has a storied history. Egyptian cultures made a practice of burying a Lapis lazuli scarab with their dead, and believed it to offer protection. The very earliest cultures valued Lapis lazuli more highly than gold. Greeks spoke of an ancient Sapphire, which was included with gold, and this was unmistakably Lapis. Some believed that dreaming of Lapis would foretell of a love that would be forever faithful.

When working or meditating with Lapis lazuli, it can bring matters more clearly to the mind. It is one of the most powerful stones and should be used with care. Wearing a Lapis lazuli ring can help you to become a channel. The ancient Egyptians used Lapis lazuli as a symbol of Truth. The main component of Lapis lazuli is jazurite (25% to 40%), a fledspathoid silicate mineral, with the formula

Royal Lapis Lazuli

(Na,Ca)8(AlSiO4)6(S,SO4,Cl)1. Most Lapis lazuli contains calcite (white), Sodalite (blue), and Pyrite (metallic yellow). Lapis lazuli usually occurs in crystalline marble as a result of contact metamorphism.

The First Position...

... Even as a baby you made people think about their actions—your arrival may even have stirred your parents on the path toward maturity. You sought to understand the actions or reactions of the world around you ever since.

The Second Position...

... As you continued to grow, people were amazed that such a young child could have such wisdom.

The Third Position...

... In your teenage years, you became more and more aware of your class, school world, and universe. Did you continue to grow and stay open or did you shut down?

The Fourth Position...

... You searched for more in your young adult years, seeking to grow beyond your childhood. Seeking to communicate to achieve better understanding was a source of joy and frustration for you during this period of time.

The Fifth Position...

... Coming to you is the awareness you have long sought.

The Sixth Position...?

... You are called upon to assume the Pharaoh and leader position in your sphere of influence, not as a god, but as a guide to the people you know to help them to grow and achieve in their lives.

Lepidolite

This stone has many applications for calmness, emotional balance, and heart healing. Lepidolite is the mineral used to derive lithium, a salt used for emotional balance and well-being. Forgive old heart wounds and allow your heart to fill once again with new love.

This stone has many applications for calmness, emotional balance and heart healing.

The type of lithium found in Lepidolite is also used to make batteries. They are one of two materials that hold onto what the emotional mental and spiritual energy they are exposed to and release "in kind" the energy they absrb.

Chemical Formula:
K(Li,Al)3(Si,Al)4O10(F,OH)2
Composition:
Molecular Weight = 388.30gm

Potassium	10.07 %	K	12.13 %	K_2O
Lithium	3.58 %	Li	7.70 %	Li_2O
Aluminum	6.95 %	Al	13.13 %	Al_2O_3
Silicon	28.93 %	Si	61.89 %	SiO_2
Hydrogen	0.26 %	H	2.32 %	H_2O
Oxygen	45.32 %	O		
Fluorine	4.89 %	F	4.89 %	F
Inert components	- %	F	2.06 %	$-O=F_2$

My ancient ancestors called this stone purple heart, for its obvious color and because it worked well on the emotional body, which was important when they had a member that was more than dysfunctional or quirky. Very often the Lepidolite would be wrapped around the head along with a piece of natural magnet (and possibly other stones). The tribal member was made to wear it until told to remove it by the stone healer. This was used as a base in combination for curing many mental disorders that are treated with drugs today, such as ADD, ADHD, depression, and memory loss. This stone is also an activator of the spiritual body or soul for someone who is closed off to God.

Lepidolite is part of the mica family (a very industrial family from which many of your daily products come from) and has perfect cleavage (ease in coming apart). The lithium aluminum silicate sheets are held together with potassium ions. Lepidolite can be found in most regions of the world.

The human body cannot operate without sufficient quantities of the minerals that make up Lepidolite, and the medicinal applications of Lithium are well documented.

The First Position...

... You brought your world a peaceful respite while you were being held as a baby and still give that to those you are closest to in intimate moments. However, since you arrived on this little ball of earth we call home, you have been a perfect mirror. You gave the people who held you as a baby a chance to reflect how the choices they have made have brought them to where they are today.

The Second Position...

… You were a very non-demanding and peaceful child while still being strong enough to stand on your "own two feet." You were probably a little power house of energy while you were a little one. Being a super sensitive you absorbed the energy in your life, home and school and then reflected the same in kind with a child's understanding. You may have struggled with "letting people in" as you got older.

The Third Position...

… The ability to quiet the storm in others may have been very useful in your junior high and high school years. If you remained open in your teenage years, you were probably a great place of rest or grace for your friends and people around you. If you built up walls to prevent feeling what other people were feeling, you were probably a little difficult to be around, unless a person was a part of your very close friends. You still possess this strength and can use it to influence or heal other people.

The Fourth Position...

... You eased into mature adulthood easier than other people. As you left your high school and childhood behind, it was like putting on a new outfit— cool but no big deal. As a young adult you want to, or wanted to, create a healing space for you to grow into. The power is within you to do it today, but it is a reflection of the growth that occurs within you.

The Fifth Position...

… Those things that you have been carrying around in your mind, body, and soul for so long will soon no longer be important. The necessity for stress will no longer be necessary—you will keep the memory but lose the pain. Hopefully you have noticed that the people around you seem to be reflecting whatever mood you are in... it's almost spooky in the sense that the world seems to be reflecting your mood... you're not crazy. You actually are absorbing and radiating the emotional, mental and spiritual energy around you. Giving back what you are getting is a choice, you can give better than you get but it will take some effort on your part. Holding or wearing a piece of this stone will help. It may now seem that people think that because they can't "stir you up," you are not moved by their situations.

The Sixth Position...?

... Meaning to the madness is on its way; the why's and the "why did this happen" will soon make sense to you. You have been carry a large load of old stuff you no longer need to hang onto, or even need look at anymore. You may free yourself of those by simply letting them go. This may be bad habits, bad memories, or regrets but may also be over-protectiveness of your children or anything else that no longer serves you and the world around you. Try it out right now... Think of something you no longer need, then simply let it dissipate.

Malachite

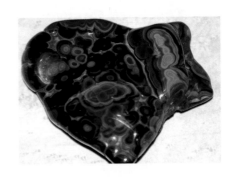

A tremendous healing and prosperity stone, Malachite draws the bearer toward her greatest need (physical healing or prosperity). However, its first priority is your wholeness. If someone is beginning a new workout, diet, and/or vitamin & mineral regiment, this stone will help to guarantee a successful outcome. Gardeners or anyone who works with the soil would be blessed by having or holding one of these stones.

Because of Malachite's strong magnetic field and the fact that it has a radiant influence based on the size of the stone (generally 100 times the size of the stone) and that it may be amplified or diminished when combined with other stones or metals, it is a good stone to be used with others for a combined or blended effect. It has a resonance of 10 and carries sound, music, and spiritual energy in a most soothing or seductive fashion. Because of this, it is difficult for the bearer to move away from it, even after it has done its work.

Facilitators and healers can use this stone to stimulate skin growth, reduce swollen tissues, and lessen the amount of scarring after injury. Carrying these same uses outside the human body, Malachite is very useful for those who work with businesses or corporations, when those corporations are suffering from overgrowth or reduction. It also has the ability to encourage people to verbalize when they would rather be withholding. Before the production of artificial pigments, it was often used to create the color green in paints and inks.

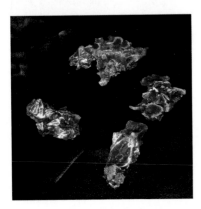

Malachite was so tied to agriculture—including farmers, fields, and orchards—that the Goddess Demeter (Greek Goddess of the Harvest) was often carved sitting on or entirely made of Malachite. Many early farming tools were fitted with a piece of Malachite. It would be an excellent gift for anyone who farms or works with the environment, or has any heart connection to another Goddess, Gaia. And it comes in many ideal gift forms, from pocket stones all the way to sculptures, as referred to above.

The First Position...

... After spending time with you as a baby, people would be very driven to change or do what they needed to be doing. You may not have been the first born, but you were the reason your parents began to move forward and/or change their lives; an example of the reason you came into this life, which is to facilitate or to help people discover the changes they need to make.

The Second Position...

… As a young child, you must have always been doing something, and it was always for the right reasons (right to you anyway). Very few people understood you, then or now.

The Third Position...

… Move on, move on, move on, experience, experience, experience was what your teenage years were about for you. You moved through your growth and changes very fast and were very moody. You didn't lose friends as quickly as you wore them out.

The Fourth Position...

...You went out on your own and away from your family because you were ready to change the world. You discovered, however, that the world wasn't ready to be changed. You may feel that you wasted time— moving from this, to this, to this. Understand, you *did* change the world and individuals you were around with each move that you made.

The Fifth Position...

… You have collected a universe of experiences. You may not have a lot of physical resources or items to show for it, but you do have a story worth telling or experience you can share with others. You enrich the lives of others simply by being in their lives with them. You are the sacred soil that allows them to grow. The more people you share your wisdom with the more prosperous you will become.

The Sixth Position...?

...If positive change hasn't happened yet it soon will ... but it is doubtful you will see this as positive. Many things look different after time has passed. Now is the time to do what is in your highest and best good. If you want to avoid "a Learning Experience," then do what your heart has always called you to do. Life will give you a continuous chance to pursue your purpose by removing those things that stand in your way or those things you choose to hide behind.

So, if you think the incident has already occurred (the learning experience), try this: If you have lost your job, go and do what you always wished you had done. If you have lost a relationship recently, focus on your growth before getting into a new one. If an accumulation of items or resources is lost, change the foundation or construct a new one. Life is trying to move you toward to what is in your highest and best good so it can place the mantle of service to yourself and/or the world on your shoulders. This will be an easy and smooth transition toward a better experience if you let it be.

Pyrite

Ruled by fire, this stone balances the male electrical energy within each person. Pyrite is used

to draw wealth and money and can be carried for good luck. It assists in manifesting ideas into creation, while bringing strength and grounding. Pyrite has also been called "Fools Gold" because many people from children to mining companies have been fooled by this gold colored material.

"Pyrite is the most common of the sulfide minerals. The name Pyrite was derived from the Greek πυρίτης (puritēs), "of fire" or "in fire," from πύρ (pur), "fire." In ancient Roman times, this name was applied to several types of stone that would create sparks when struck against steel. Pliny the Elder described one of them as being brassy, almost certainly a reference to what *we* now call pyrite. By Georgius Agricola's time, the term had become a generic term for all of the sulfide minerals.

Pyrite is usually found associated with other sulfides or in Quartz veins, sedimentary rock, and metamorphic rock, as well as in coal beds, and as a replacement mineral in fossils. Despite being nicknamed fool's gold, Pyrite is sometimes found in association with small quantities of Gold. Gold and arsenic occur as a coupled substitution in the Pyrite structure. In the Carlin, Nevada Gold deposit, Arsenian Pyrite contains up to 0.37 wt %Gold. Auriferous Pyrite is a valuable ore of Gold." (from Wikipedia)

Contrary to its epithet of Fool's Gold, Pyrite has been used in the development of technology for many hundreds of years. It was used to create a spark to fire early rifles, it was used in some of the earliest mineral detectors, it helped to make semi-conductors possible, and has become invaluable in the production of inexpensive solar panels, and therefore in the growth of that industry.

Ancient teachers and healers used Pyrite to treat many conditions. It helped the early healers hone their skills to determine and better understand what minerals and other items the body needs for better health. To do this, the healer would use a cube, sun, or wand of Pyrite to spiritually and intellectually connect with the person receiving treatment. The deep conductive aspects of Pyrite would also be useful for a priest, shaman, or counselor to connect with someone in deep rehabilitation or in his jail ministry. If someone was Vitamin D deficient or suffered from winter/weather related depression, Pyrite would give them that sun worshipper energy without the sunburn. A simple pendent or wire-wrapped piece of jewelry would be sufficient.

The First Position...

... You were a highly active and alert baby. You would go and go—and then nap anywhere that was available in that moment, then get up and go and go some more.

The Second Position...

… You were a bundle of energy and loved to explore, constantly grabbing life and lifting it up to see what was under it. You were all about energy, yours and what source of energy anything else had.

The Third Position...

… It wasn't as important for you to learn "a thing" as much as you wanted to know about the "energy or force" behind it. Your mind is constantly active, and I hope you found some way to keep it stimulated … or you did and do find life rather boring.

The Fourth Position...

... Leaving home was more about discovering what was out there than what you were leaving behind. Understanding your push or drive was almost as important as discovering the force or energy behind everything else. If you have something that has to get done, you'll work until it is done or until exhaustion overtakes you.

The Fifth Position...

… You are or can be life to others, but you need to re-charge your batteries too. You have the ability to warm and radiate to others. This is a skill you have. You can use this positively or negatively—you can warm the lives of others or hit them with it.

The Sixth Position...?

...An opportunity for prosperity is coming at you. The opportunity will come at you energetically first, maybe as a great idea that you have to do. Maybe this will come through something you have been praying for or meditating on—or maybe through an e-mail. Be alert to catch it because it's electric and fast.

Quartz

I could do an entire reading using nothing but variations of quartz. I could name 50 easily and there is no such thing as just "Plain Ole Quartz." So, let me talk to you about plain old Quartz.

Nothing that generates a frequency can operate without Quartz. In fact, nothing that is electric or computerized can either. Silica is the basis of our planet; it is Quartz by another name and (some would argue) the foundation of all life on our planet. So, if you took Silica/Quartz off our planet, what would be left wouldn't make up a large asteroid.

Nearly everything referred to as crystal—all clear gems, and everything that grows in the classic crystalline shape—is some variation of Quartz. It is the second most common geological form, the first being feldspar. However, most of the Quartz being used by technology and industry today is "lab grown" because it gives them more consistency, NOT better Quartz.

That is not to say that Quartz by itself isn't beautiful. Plain old Quartz has been faceted as gems, worn in crowns, placed on scepters and thrones, and carved into gods, goddesses, and goblets. Quartz has adorned the castles of kings and the homes of the wealthy since it was first discovered many, many thousands of years ago.

Being energetically connected to Quartz, you should want to understand it. Yes, I did just say "you are energetically connected to Quartz." You are energetically affected all the time by the Quartz around you—whether it's the gemstone ring you wear, the jewels in your watch, the crystal in your iPod, or the Quartz you are walking above, science has proven you are subject to vibration and therefore to Quartz. Although, the piezoelectric effect of Quartz is what made the old phonograph needles (of Quartz) react, I would not be the first person to call you a great big walking crystal and therefore affected in the same way.

So here is what we teach on the cards we hand out about clear Quartz crystal. "A glowing crystal is the ancient symbol for the light of the spirit. It promotes harmony, balance, clarity, and perfection. Quartz crystal is used to amplify, clarify, and store energy. It radiates energy called the piezoelectric effect.

Quartz crystals (silicone dioxide) are formed naturally from silicone and water through heat and pressure. A crystal takes over 10,000 years to form and most are 100–125 million years old. Most crystals form in a hexagon formation, the six sides symbolize the six chakras and the top termination point corresponds to the crown chakra that connects you to the infinite."

The First Position...

... Recently I was walking down the streets of Boston when I saw a lady who had the hardest time getting down the street—not because of any kind of dysfunction, but because she was holding a baby that everyone wanted to get a peek at. Oh sure it was a cute baby but no cuter than most. Upon contemplation I realized it was a crystal child. Like you, this baby reminds us of our light within. You as a baby reminded us of our own fountain of light. You came into this life to accomplish something specific—probably had something to do with bringing something out of the shadows and into the light, maybe as an inventor or with a new way of looking at things.

The Second Position...

... You were a something as a child—and I don't mean this in a derogatory sense. You may have been an organizer of games, or maybe you liked to hug people. Maybe you were the one that got kids to be friends. You symbolized harmony, balance, or clarity which may have annoyed some but most respected it. Your natural curiosity could have taken a lot of forms as a child, and so you were at least interesting to have around. You had a natural desire to want to make things better.

My Partner standing with "JUST" a piece of quartz

The Third Position...

… You refracted the light. You could have shown people the rainbow or recombined it into white light. You may have shown many faces to many people (as the need arose) or you were a regular beacon of white light drawing from the sources around you. You were or are the kind of person who questions and/or changes everything from the inside out. You had or may still have an unspoken desire or are blatant and upfront.

The Fourth Position...

...You left your adolescence and birth family to chase your own rainbow. You probably hopped around for a while until you found the color that suited you best and (hopefully) stuck to that path. Your desire was or is to do things differently than they have been done before through enlightening your own life with knowledge and creating a better way, inside the things you are already involved in.

The Fifth Position...

… You have or you are about to bring all the parts of yourself back together to form a consistent beam forward for the rest of your life. You may become a beacon that helps others find their way or become a wide radiating beam so that all around you can enjoy the light you give. You are either about to or are already offering the world around you the benefit of your experience... Are you writing a book? Working as a mentor (boss, manager, or teacher) of younger people? These would be positive uses of crystal energy surrounding your life right now.

The Sixth Position...?

...You are going to have the opportunity to achieve better clarity and empowerment. You can choose how you learn this. You can pick the path of service or "a learning experience." This all important lesson is before you—you may choose how you learn the lesson. Your hard drive is about to get downloaded. You are going to get a load of information to integrate into your life. This could be through a book, message, or change in life path. This can be completely painless if you are willing to receive it.

Rhodochrosite

this beautiful pink (and white) stone helps the user to manifest new love in life. All for expansion of heart energies and connect with universal love. Therapeutically, it is excellent for someone who is suffering from rheumatoid arthritis or sports injury to the tissues and ligaments around joints. Can be found in nearly every time zone. Gem quality is VERY rare.

In the soup mother nature calls rhodochrosite ($MnCO_3$), she has combined manganese with carbon and an a pinch of some iron, magnesium, calcium, zinc, and cobalt occasionally. She cooked up a stone version of an aphrodisiac. Is it interesting that the body cannot sustain good health without magnesium and calcium, the emotional body wilts without love, the spiritual body dies without faith and the intellect does grow without fascination. Mother nature brought us a gourmet meal of all of the above in this wonderful stone. (internal consumption is not a god idea).

The First Position...

... People must have loved holding you, it's a wonder you ever learned to walk. You were a radiator of the force of the universe... Love. And you still can be. Being a love warrior or ambassador doesn't mean you have to be a doormat and/or let people rub the "stuff" off on to you. Shining the light of love on situations where you or others aren't being treated as they should be can be a wondrous gift... or ... you can just begin to feel it for yourself again.

The Second Position...

... You were probably a very active toddler and young child but not active as a lightning bolt, more like a butterfly. You help to spread connection and commonality wherever you went.

The Third Position...

... it must have been very hard for you to see kids being mean to each other when you were a teenager. However the people that you were close to in those years still think fondly of you to this day. You were the one person people could be around that made them feel whole or accepted.

The Fourth Position...

... The moving away from your family (if you actually did move away) must have felt like you were being pushed out of the nest and told to "fly". Did you ever tell your family about how this felt? This maybe the time to do so....

The Fifth Position...

… Love and service that you have shared with others will be returning to you. AND, you will not have to work so hard to find it in your world. So, don't try so hard, let it happen.

The Sixth Position...?

... Hold on tight and strengthen who you are emotionally. Love and service that you have shared with others will be returning to you. AND, you will not have to work so hard to find it in your world. So, don't try so hard, let it happen.

Localities for Rhodochrosite **Map taken from http://www.mindat.org/min-3406.html**

Rose Quartz

Much of what was said in the chapter on Quartz also pertains to this pink sister. It gently allows you to feel the allness of Love, which is the essence of the universe. It calms the mind and emotional body, releasing concerns or worries. Because of this, it is extremely soothing to young children or anyone who suffers maladies of the heart. Facilitators can use this to help their clients to feel the Power of the Universe and those that meditate with it will feel the Power of Love as well...more strongly in gem form.

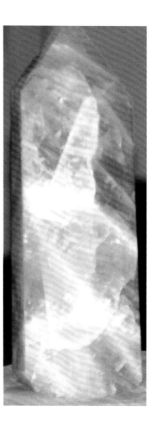

The First Position...

... From the time you came into this world all you did (or wanted too) was bathe the world in love (or wanted too). Everyone who held you felt reminded of what it felt like to be loved. You have the ability to radiate this love to everyone, but you have difficulty expressing it toward a specific individual. They feel it so strongly from you that they know you are sending it, but you may not be sending it specifically to them. As an example—we breathe air, but does air breathe? You radiate love—do you feel it?

The Second Position...

… You showed love to all the world around you as a young child. You might have been the target of bullies or children with other bad behavior because they were craving the energy you were projecting. I hope you had someone watching out for you.

The Third Position...

… As an emissary of love, you attracted a lot of the people who really needed to feel love. Some of that was good, some of that was bad, and some was mean or worse. You may have attracted a protector, which was nice to have back then. You don't need one now.

The Fourth Position...

... You probably left home by beginning a marriage or some other smooth way to do it. One of your parents may have tried very hard to hang onto you. In each area and/or phase in your life, you found one person who was protective/very supportive/clingy, or in other words, a bit of a shadow because he or she really liked being around you.

The Fifth Position...

... You are going (and may have already begun) to learn to love your world... all of it and everything in it. There are two great emotional energies that guide us and all that is—Love and Impel. We all know when we are encouraging out of love or when we are impelling someone. Love is about allowing; impel is about force or en-forcing. Since you have agreed to learn this great lesson, and since there are only two ways people learn anything, either through service or pain, choose service because it is a better way.

The Sixth Position...?

… You are now or you are about to enter a very sweet place. The energy surrounding your life is becoming supportive and compassionate love. If you will not resist it and release worry you can enjoy this period of support that the universe is going to rain down on you. If you are called to release something, do so with an open hand so the universe can replace it with something better.

Ruby in Fuchsite

... creates an openness around the emotion part of our lives, Gives the bearer the confidence to speak their truth and makes someone uncomfortable when they are not telling the truth. Stimulates the use of electrolytes in the brain and makes memory more clear. Helps the growth of faith and so, helps in the application of someone's spiritual path.

Ruby in Fuchsite is excellent at breaking through hard emotional and spiritual walls. I sneak a piece of this into every pouch of the workshops I do. By the time the attendees have worn this for a few hours they are extremely ready to get at what is holding them back.... and I don't tell them what is for or what it will do until after the session.

Fuchsite $KAl_2(Si_3Al)O_{10}(OH,F)_2$ = Potassium, Aluminum, Silicon enriched with Aluminum, Oxygen, Oxygen & Hydrogen with a dash of Flourine.

Ruby: Al_2O_3 = Aluminum and Oxygen.

When mother nature put these two substances together she created a super salve for the emotional and mental bodies. People and animals have literally died of a broken heart where no other physical reason explains why they have passed. Grief has caused many aged seniors to join their recently passed life partner for no other physical explanation. Ancient guru and healers made war widows medallions out of ruby in fuchsite, so that they could heal and move forward.

Almost everyone has endured the agony that comes from true emotional pain, let this awesome stone bring you back to wholeness instead of building walls to which the wonder of you get's hidden behind.

The First Position...

... Oh how you sparkled and shined as an infant. Your sweetness and emotions just delightfully spilled all over anyone who held you. You made people giggle just by looking at you.

The Second Position...

... You were a very sensitive child. You picked up other energy and emotions around you and then radiated them. As you got a little older you could pick out if someone was hurting or was having a hard time and would do what you could to comfort them.

The Third Position...

... As a teenager you weren't good at hiding how you felt. You could look very dreamy or longingly at someone you cared for, and that wasn't always understood but, their was no mistaking if they upset you or were mean. You may have held your emotions very near the surface but the people who knew you, also knew they could share with you because you made them feel better.... And you still have all of these gifts and traits.

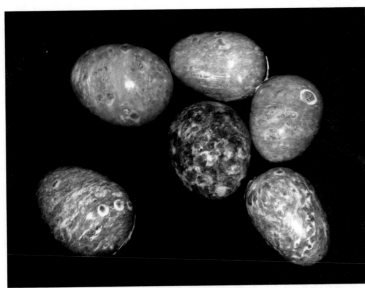

The darker green egg in the center is also refered to as Zoisite, the drker green is made so by the pressence of iron.

The Fourth Position...

... You left your childhood and family behind because you were tired of all the fakes, flakes and drama. You needed to find truth even if it was just your truth.

The Fifth Position...

... You need to open up, to drop the walls. Those walls served you a while ago... Now they just keep you behind them and make you unable to connect. Anger, hurt and frustration, no longer have to be a part of your reality. But, since that is what your walls are made out of... that is what your SPECIAL SPICE is to every situation.

The Sixth Position...?

... More openness, love and communication are coming your way. Are you open and ready for it?

Selenite

Selenite aligns all bodies and becomes a highway for travel to other realms. It symbolizes the clearest state of mind attainable. Excellent for telepathic communication, it. combines well with Herkimer and Celestite. Selenite is an alternate name for the mineral gypsum. The word selenite comes from the Greek "selenites," meaning "moon stone" or "moon rock," with the root word "Selene" meaning "Moon," and for good reason—the mineral selenite is the near transparent and colorless crystal form of gypsum, which

exudes a pearly lustre that glows and can very much resemble the moon. Selene is also the name of the Greek Goddess of the Moon.

Gypsum is a common sedimentary mineral—the most common of all the sulfates—and is usually found in massive beds of tabular or block crystal form. These sedimentary deposits are formed through a hastened acceleration of evaporating saline water, and in the process, may retain trapped bubbles of either air or water called "enhydros." Gypsum is often found in caves, in evaporated lakes or sea beds, or salt flats. It is interesting to note that if the natural conditions become extremely dry and the gypsum becomes overly dehydrated, it transforms into the mineral known as anhydrite. If water is then reintroduced, it is restored back into gypsum.   There are five main types of gypsum, known by the following names: Selenite, Satin Spar (not to be confused with Iceland Spar, which is a related Calcite), Gypsum Flower, Desert Rose, and Alabaster. The first four crystalline varieties are commonly known as Selenite even though they contain some notable differences in appearance. The larger crystalline form of Selenite, being a clear colorless crystal, is rarer than the other forms of the mineral. Satin Spar is usually fibrous, translucent white and satiny. The other forms of gypsum are readily available in tabular, rosette, or needle-like crystals, with Alabaster being the granular massive form of the mineral. Selenite crystals can be quite large, but the mineral itself is very soft and slightly flexible (although not elastic, meaning it can be bent but will not resume its original shape on its own). Often fibrous, it can be easily broken or scratched. In fact, all forms of gypsum are soft (between 1 1/2 and 2 on the Mohs Scale) and can be scratched with just a fingernail. As a form of gypsum, Selenite is a natural insulator and will appear much warmer to the touch than other crystals. Industrial grades of gypsum are used in making sheet rock drywall, concrete, and Plaster of Paris. Both Selenite and Satin

Spar are often vitreous (glassy), pearly, and silky to the touch, and both may exhibit chatoyancy (cat's eye reflections). They also both contain a fiber optic quality, have the ability to double refract, and some specimens are fluorescent or phosphorescent. Gypsum Flowers, Desert Roses, and Alabasters are usually not as lustrous, and often will have a gritty appearance. In very dry areas, sand becomes trapped within and on the surface of the forming crystals, and often these inclusions are seen as shapes, such as the common "hourglass" shape found on Selenite crystals in the Great Salt Plains lakebed. The Desert Rose variety is shaped like a rose as its name suggests, its "petals" formed by overlapping blades of Selenite. They are often a dusty rose, reddish, or brown color. With their softness and natural formation related to water, all of the gypsum varieties should never be left standing in any liquid, and all cleansers should be avoided, as the water will degrade and eventually dissolve the mineral, while soaps and cleansers will affect any luster.

Selenite is neither magnetic or carries or exhibits a frequency of it's own... that doesn't mean it isn't powerful. It does for frequency, current or magnetism what water does for soup. As soup carries and enhances all the spices and flavors combined with it selenite does the same with; sound, lights, frequencies and energy... Not just a one to one ratio but, it enhances exponentially any form of light, frequency or energy exposed to it.

 A famous location for Selenite blades is the Naica Mine in Chihuahua, Mexico and is called the "Cave of Swords." Here giant crystals have formed, some measuring over 30 feet long. A fairly common mineral, Selenite can be found throughout the world.

Selenite is neither a carrier of frequency nor magnetic, but that doesn't mean that it isn't powerful. Selenite is Mother Nature's fiber optic and transfers well the energies that are placed on it or next to it. It makes a great base for a talisman because it only radiates what stones you "spice" it with. Larger pieces also can cast and receive as well as a satellite dish. Selenite wands are good for sending Reiki or other healing energies, and they are also good for scanning to see problem areas.

Selenite is a great wedding stone and was used by ancient American peoples to bond a couple by having them hold it together for the first week because it would pick up and share the love and energy of each one for the other.

The First Position...
... You were born into this world to help bring people and their many aspects together.

The Second Position...
... You were a delightful young child as you responded to nature's sweet song. Sometimes others saw it as a sour note. Nevertheless, you still help people find the lost parts of their soul with your spiritual connection.

The Third Position...
... Your gifts as a natural networker began to flower and bloom in the middle and high school years. Your ability to connect and see what is "really going on" still serves you today.

The Fourth Position...
...As you left your childhood behind and moved into a more adult phase of your path, you were looking to connect to some new source, to get more of what you need, and/or to pull up a new source of support for your life.

The Fifth Position...
... The universe is sending; are you receiving? Are you open to signs, wonders, and the messages around you? Whatever question, experience, or knowledge you seek, you need only to be open to it.

The Sixth Position...?
... Life is sustaining you and will continue to do so. You can worry over it if you want, but if you do, you won't improve or dissolve the support the universe is sending to you. You made decisions a long time ago that have set the tone for now. Your life is sustained as the trees in the forest so you don't need a gardener. You can garden the trees if you want, but it will not help them (nor will it hurt them either.)

Serpentine

Aids in concentration and Life force, is a vitality enhancer. It snakes its way through your mental area bringing you strength in hard or confrontational situations. Enables you to discover the truth in situations on an intuitive level and (for some people) enhances your gifts of discernment. It is also a binder and protector from psychic attacks and other negative energies. Oh, and looks very cool carved or in a natural setting on your desk at work.

Shown as its name in most stores and the color is usually seen as a pea to hunter (dark forest) green. It has jagged or squiggly lines running through it of lighter and darker material. The more translucent or gem like serpentine has a shiny to waxy appearance, while the more opaque or stone like appear to have a natural polished to them. Roman, Greek and Pagan healers would tell their patrons to drink from from cups made of serpentine to extend their lives. Ancient to recent sculptures made from serpentine are symbols of strength, vitality and of life. Apparently these ancients peoples knew before we did. The formula begins with Deuterium and is linked to longer life, Formula $D_2[Si_2O_5](OH)_4$.

"Dr Shchepinov's theory is based on deuterium, a naturally-occurring isotope, or form of hydrogen, that strengthens the bonds in between and around the body's cells, making them less vulnerable to attack. He found that water enriched with deuterium, which is twice as heavy as normal hydrogen, extends the lifespan of worms by 10 per cent. And fruitflies fed the 'water of life' lived up to 30 per cent longer"

Read more: http://www.dailymail.co.uk/sciencetech/article-1089710/Its-time-raise-glass-heavy-water-longer-life.html#ixzz2WIedsQzp
Follow us: @MailOnline on Twitter | DailyMail on Facebook

Serpentine has also been used as shields in nuclear reactors, different types of Serpentine (of which there are many) have been used to filter air and water to remove poison and particulate... There is even some speculation that the Mars atmosphere could be turned to breathable air through serpenization. Antigorite (a type of fibrous serpentine) can be used to strengthen concrete and make it last longer.

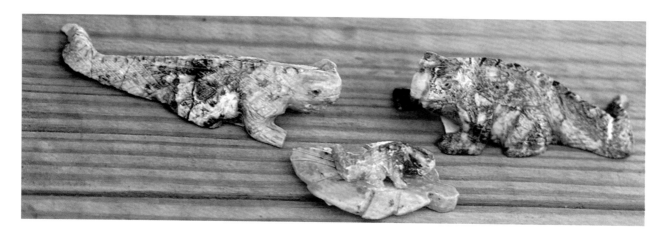

The First Position...

... You were probably a very active baby that didn't care to be held by a lot of strangers. Most people felt revitalized after having held you, but you may not have been very fun to try to hold onto.

The Second Position...

... I'm sure you were an active child. Finding out how something worked was important to you and may have even gotten you into a little trouble when you were a child. You are a very tactile learner. So you learn better by doing than by hearing about it or watching someone else do it.

The Third Position...

... School was probably very difficult for you because they wanted you to learn by talking at you. You have always had a talent for figuring things out and fixing things that are broken (sometimes you were the one that broke them). Friendships, in school. May have been difficult for you because people are harder to fix and some people do not want to be... fixed that is.

The Fourth Position...

... You needed to venture out to create or make some future for your self. It wasn't so much about drama, emotion or anything intangible... Make, create, do... that is what you were all about. Your were ready to take your world and turn it into something.

The Fifth Position...

... Time for you to start your biggest project ever, YOU. You have spent a good portion of your time fixing, repairing, working on, empowering and shielding others. All the while working with a limp, or rather, still being injured yourself... Now it's time and you have felt this coming. Maybe you wouldn't have said or implied it this way but, now it is time to fix you.

The Sixth Position...?

... You are now or you soon will be stepping into a powerful place in at least a couple areas of your life. I think this is a blessing, but not everyone sees it that way. You are becoming "In Command" where your decisions and thoughts will be acted on by others both seen and unseen. But remember, to whom much is given much is expected.

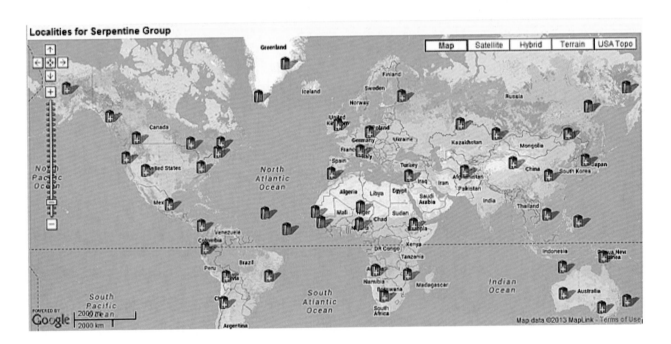

Shiva Lingam

Lingam Stones are found in the Mandhata Mountains, one of India's seven sacred places of pilgrimage. Each stone has Tantric markings symbolic of the marks on Lord Shiva's forehead. They are said to contain the highest vibration of all stones

on Earth and assist in purifying the temple or home environment. Most sandstone is considered fairly dead (non-energetic material). However since it is actually microscopic pieces of Quartz bonded together, and it vibrates with the frequency of Om. The Mandhata range has more sacred sites than any other 100 square miles on the planet. Some of these sacred sites date back many thousands of years. In ancient times, the stones were drawn out of the Ganges River, after having fallen off the mountain range, and would be tumbled in and polished by the fine sands of the river for many miles. Then the Shiva Lingam were drawn out of the river by Vedics and Gurus and were thought to have been radiators of Prana (the red), Tantra (the tan) and Kundalini energy (grayish color); the latter representing its integration into the earth's physical plane. In modern times these stones are mined and shaped to keep up with the demand of a global marketplace, which doesn't negate the power or energy of the stone—it only affects the romantic story attached to Shiva Lingam. Many people believe these are sexual symbols. Certainly, if you incorporate and focus the energies of Prana, Tantra, or Kundalini within your passion you will have a "mindblowing" experience, but there is a lot more to it than that. There are the many Gods of India, and there seems to be a different story relating to Shiva Lingam for every God there is in India. Each story, though, is in some way connected to one of the greatest of their elder Gods, Shiva.

The original was said to be created by the Indian Goddess Parvati by shaping the sand from the Kanchipuram region of India and then worshipping Shiva. Temples were built around or near Swayambus (sacred rock formation outcroppings). There are Shiva Lingam that appeared all on their own, untouched by human hands. One appears every year at the end of a glacier, and still others are pre-date any of history's calendars.

The energy of the Shiva Lingam can be used to vitalize many aspects of a person's life; the position it falls on in the reading adds punch to wherever it lands.

The First Position...
Your arrival revitalized your birth family and caused them to refocus. When people held you, you revitalized them. You have, since childhood, added power to whatever groups you were involved in.

The Second Position...
You were a fun toddler with your constant activity and buzzing energy and to this day, you are a physically affectionate individual (as long as it wasn't trained out of you).

The Third Position...
… The Shiva Lingam teenager is highly intelligent, very connected, philosophical, and affectionate. These can add to a person's popularity or distract from it.

The Fourth Position...
… You began to build a world away from your childhood through a desire to add to the substance of your life. You are looking to express and draw vibrancy to your life.

The Fifth Position...
… You are moving to a level of intimacy with yourself and to a deeper understanding of the people around you.

The Sixth Position...?
… You are coming to a sense of yourself and your place in the Universe. This is one of the deepest understandings you can come to have and if you simply allow this to come, you can become like the Magi or High Priests of old. If you resist it and/or fight it, this experience can embitter you.

YES! It IS, and they even get bigger than this!

Smokey Quartz

This smokey form of Quartz represents our deep unconscious and teaches us to be realistically grounded spiritually. Excellent for stability, strength, and grounding, Smoky Quartz is a popular variety of Quartz. It has an unusual color for a gemstone and is easily recognized and well-known by the general public. It is an excellent stone for someone or a group recovering from substance abuse or to simply change bad attitudes. And it is also an excellent therapy stone for willfulness, anger, or forgiveness. Large pieces are said to make you feel "safe enough" or protected enough to release any major issue.

Smoky Quartz, itself a variety of Quartz, has a few varieties of its own.

1. Cairngorm is a variety that comes from the Cairngorm Mountains in Scotland.

2. Morion is a very dark black opaque variety of Smoky Quartz from India and Madagascar.

3. Coon Tail Quartz from Arkansas is a Smoky Quartz with an alternating black and gray banding.

4. A Gwindel, found in Europe, is a Smoky Quartz cluster of nearly parallel crystals, each rotated slightly relative to the one beside it.

The color of Smoky Quartz is variable from brown to black and sometimes smoky gray colored specimens are included as Smoky Quartz. The cause of the color of Smoky Quartz is in question but it is almost certainly related to the amount of exposure to radiation that the stone has undergone. Natural Smoky Quartz often occurs in granitic rocks that have a small but persistent amount of radioactivity. Most Smoky Quartz that makes its way to rock shops and to some gem cutters has been artificially irradiated to produce a dark black color.

Natural Smoky Quartz comes from many sources around the world. A few of the more noteworthy locations include Brazil, the world's largest supplier; the Pikes Peak area of Colorado, US, where it is associated with Green Amazonite and the Swiss Alps, Arkansas, and India, which has produced many tons of fine specimens.

The brown and black Smokey Quartz wasn't always worn as a spiritual token. The Apache and Aztec warriors would turn larger pieces into knives and wear them in a concealed place (similar to the Scottish sgian dubhs) and smaller chip shards would be tied to the fingertips as wolf or jaguar claws. Early warriors were drawn to these stone for the sharpness, hardness, and the sense of protection it seemed to engender.

The First Position
You helped people to feel **really good** when they held you as a baby. You gave them an almost indescribable feeling of wholeness... not just loved, but entire and together. Even today, people you are very close to get this from you, those that can not accept it may accuse you of judging them and you don't know what they are talking about.

The Second Position
You developed the ability to know or understand things much earlier than other children. You were a good child that did all the practical things you should have done or you absolutely understood when you weren't and therefore frustrated those in authority around you. This gift from this age either allows you to nail people or allows you to free them with your words... It is almost a power you have with the use of your voice.

The Third Position
You were who you were as a teenager. You may have "followed the crowd" but it is because you choose to. You have had the ability to pick something up or leave it alone since you were a teenager. You can start or stop at will, by simply deciding to. Which also allowed you to be the one that people could count on when they needed to.

The Forth Position
You moved away from home when it was the best thing to do for everyone involved. You make decisions based on practical considerations because that works for you.

The Fifth Position

Life is changing for you... like the path has already been laid and you are just coasting into it. Examine this closely, make sure this IS what you want. Allow it if it is... If not, apply the brakes and change lanes.

The Sixth Position

WHOA...! You want to stop right now and assess the direction of your path. Eventhough it looks the same as it has for some time, step carefully and make sure the path is solid... Examine all areas of your life... If everything is happening as you want it, then proceed. If not, then now is the time for adjustment.

Sodalite

...Sodalite gives us access to our intuitive abilities and our subconscious mind. The stone enhances our mental performance by bringing up images from the subconscious. Helpful during meditation and journeys in understanding your life path.

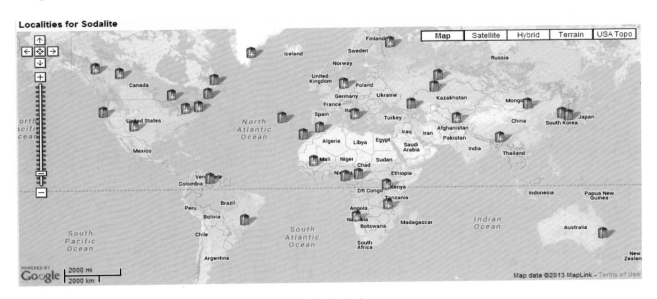

Map obtained from http://www.mindat.org/min-3701.html

     This is a beautiful material with high amounts of Sodium (hence the name sodalite). It was first discovered around 1877 and become a popular stone for jewelry when larger deposits were found 20 years later. Sodalite can be found most regions of the world. Its gem grade isn't always a vibrant blue. The gem grades range from a grayish white through (most of the) blue and purple ranges and sometimes pink. Some varieties have been known to change color based on the light they are stored or displayed in. Sodalite changes color to an orange under blacklight.

It's formula is $Na_8 (Al_6 Si_6 O_{24}) Cl_2$, It's a hard a material but breaks apart easier than the hardness would lead you to believe.

Sodalite is good for the emotional body (as most salt minerals are). When someone is faced with continuous competition or a confrontational environment, sodalite settles the emotional body and allows it to pass through these situations like a boat powers through a storm. Good for sales people, police officers and diplomats. They won't get rocked by other people's opinions of them.

Sodalite is good for the mental body toward concentration and focus. Helps an individual zero in and find their "zone."

Spiritually sodalite brings out faith and bravery.

The First Position...

... Have you ever been around anyone that made you feel good just to be around them? Since childhood, you have had the ability to inspire optimism in those that are around you and, even more, when you first got here and people held you for the first time.

The Second Position...

… You were very busy trying to figure things out as a young child and didn't like to be bothered by other peoples' considerations. You got very interested in things that interested you or you went and "discovered" what would interest you.

The Third Position...

… Everyone had a few friends back in the mid-grades and high school but you were not easy to be a friend with or made friends easily. You challenged the way people think about things. You may have even developed a confrontational streak back then - that may still be true today.

The Fourth Position...

... Part of sodalite is the discovery of yourself. Having it show in this position means that is what you were trying to do as you moved away from your childhood friends and family. Having it show up here also means you left something important behind you. Work with the energy of sodalite to find out what worked for you then so you can bring it back into your life now..

The Fifth Position...

... It's time to get on with it, You may already know what "IT" is... and if you don't, the next step is finding out what "it" is: Your calling and why you came. It may not be a change in occupation as much as it is a change in direction.

The Sixth Position...?

... Belief, faith and hope are all here or coming to you. Try it, risk it and it will be rewarded... Not just an answer but divine action is coming for or to you.

Sunstone

...is a form of Peach colored feldspar. It works well to align the second and third chakras. It offers benevolent use of power by illuminating the motives of others and helps bring one into their personal power. It also helps us use our gifts in the service to others.

Sunstone because of it's peachy and chunky feldspar makeup has a gem that is very near that same peachy coloration.

There are many flavors or moods of sunstone but what is most common in the metaphysical and rocks shops is one that is about as big as your thumb with 1mm to 3mm little jemmy peach colored chips in it.

The recipe of the mineral soup that made this pretty stone is calcium, sodium, aluminum, silicate... I think when calcite was the dominant fluid on our planet, the calcium dissolved pockets of sodium and aluminum that were incorporated into super heated silica sands slow cooked by mother nature over the millennia, to then be discovered by us.

There are many unscientific statements that copper is in this feldspar. I have no evidence to establish this and where stones have copper in them they are generally green or blue... not peach.

There are even some exciting sunstone gems out of Oregon where the peach is suspended inside of a clear outer matrix. (like a treasure crystal). The dynamic and deep coloration of these stones is said to be a direct relationship to red copper inclusions with the stone, but I have not tested any of these in my lab, nor can I find any collaboration of this claim.

Sunstone is good for the physical because it can be laid on any of the 12 meridians to revitalize them. Like other stones with salt, it is good for mental functioning. Faith, belief and hope all enhance the spiritual body. The combination of the spiritual and mental has led people to have good luck in games of chance because it heightens the intellect to make you more observant.

The First Position...

... People perceived you as a pretty bright eyed baby because you made them feel good about themselves. You gave an extra boost to those that were creative and/or artistic. Throughout your life you could have been a muse to any one you knew who was creative.

The Second Position...

... You were probably a good little helper to everyone around you when you were a small child. A willingness and ability to help or serve is a gift.

The Third Position...

… It's easy to hand a capable person "things to do." You probably found yourself with a lot of chores to do as a teenager and/or helped your friends with things they had to do. This may also have translated into adulthood with an ability to take on a project and get it done.

The Fourth Position...

… You may have gotten tired of handling other peoples "stuff" or simply rolled into your own responsibilities without much "right of passage" or fan fare. However being capable doesn't mean you should be handling other peoples' situations.

The Fifth Position...

… There are certain things one gains from being the person everyone can come to, but there are also anchors involved. The balance for you now is to shift those responsibilities onto the people you have been handling life for and to free yourself up to address your core and your needs. If you have already been doing this, then you need to start doing things/projects and other areas of importance for you.

The Sixth Position...?

… You have been holding onto some aspect of your life (with other people) way too tightly, and you are right to assume that it might slip away. This can be family, personal, business or financial but, you can not stop it from slipping away. The tighter you hang on to prevent this, the more damage you will do. The more you vest into holding onto it, the least of it you will redeem. It's going away. The forces pulling it are greater than you can muster to stop it. If you simply release it, most of it will return to you eventually. If you go with it (go with the flow), you will end up better off on the other side of it.

Tiger's Eye

This stone, a form of Quartz, ranges in color from red, brown and gold to cream, black and blue. It assists in organizing details into a coherent whole and enhances clear perception and insight.

Tiger's Eye has a soothing effect and can be used for grounding and stabilizing. It also helps to release fear and enhances optimism, furthering one's openness to life.
The composition of Tiger's Eye is a chatoyant (fibrous) gemstone consisting of Quartz with parallel veins of silicified, altered Crocidolite that is converted into or impregnated with Silica. It is the Limonite ($FeO(OH) \cdot nH2O$) that is what primarily creates the color of gold in Tiger's Eye. Iron and nitrogen combine to assist in the growth of awareness, thus making this stone helpful in business and for personal prosperity. Many of the ancient healers and magi refered to them as Sunbeam and the Blue Tiger's Eye as Moonbeam because they noted the enhanced awareness or en-light-enment.

The First Position...
... You were a baby whose eyes were always darting about and taking in the whole room. You were a very active and fun toddler, unless someone was trying to catch you or get you to take a nap— you had lots of energy.

The Second Position...
... You liked to put things together (and sometimes take things apart). You were a great helper, and you still like to fix whatever is broken... even if they do not want you to.

The Third Position...
... Shows you to be a warrior or defender in your teenage years, but you still have these urges while finding ways to help to smooth things or situations out.

The Fourth Position...
... You sprang out of your adolescence seeking to set you own foundation and as an agent of your own interest. Opportunities simply fell or have fallen into your lap in these young adult years.

The Fifth Position...
... You are being called upon to become aware of your life and where it is now! You can change the course or direction of any of the 12 areas of your existence. This is not necessarily a good place to start from scratch, but rather is a place to "pick-up where you left off."

The Sixth Position...?
... A new opportunity awaits but you must be watching for it. If a new course of direction or a way to boost who or where you are in life should come along... DO IT! It will revitalize you.

Tiger's Eye Blue

...This stone (also refereed to as Hawk's Eye), consists of closely packed parallel crocidolite fibers that have been permeated and/or partially replaced by virtually colorless micro-crystalline quartz, black to blue. It assists in the observation of details into a coherent whole and enhances clear perception and insight.

Hawk's Eye gives some people the ability to break down spiritual concepts in easy to understand chunks for themselves or others. Realization of faith or to bring your dreams or vision into reality, is also a benefit that a person could get from meditating or wearing Hawk's Eye.

Hawk's Eye gives others the mental ability to view things from a more elevated position so they can get or possess "the big picture".

The First Position...

... Many babies have eyes that dart around but even when you were first born you would focus on something and look very closely at it. You still have the gift of focus... you just have to trust it.

The Second Position...

... As a toddler you loved to watch things and, if it fascinated you, you would jump in to see if it was fun. It was kind of dangerous then and only a little safer now. Be sure to look before you leap or at least stick just your toe in first.

The Third Position...

... You have always been a very visual person. And If you didn't see it, you didn't see it! I 'm not just talking about your eyesight. If you didn't see the point, you didn't care about it. So, you probably had trouble with subjects you didn't see the point in, when you were in school. Even to this day, if someone will take the time to explain the importance of "it". You are great at "IT".

The Fourth Position...

... When it came time for you to leave home, younger or older. You wanted to see what you could see and get where you could get. You were sort of a "rolling stone" at first and even in college you would have changed majors a lot. Being able to move quickly and see other opportunities can be a gift if it is used properly.

The Fifth Position...
... WOAH!!! STOP! Get high above this situation so you can look at it from an elevated position. You need to see what is coming and what is coming together. You are making decisions with a limited line of view and you need to expand your sources of information. I'm not saying that someone is or isn't lying to you but, that you need more information on what is going on.

The Sixth Position...?
... Something will or is coming up quick on the horizon and you will need to make a decision to be a part of it or get out of the way. There is a change that will take place, but you have to decide if you want to be a part of the change or not.

Tiger's Eye Red

… (sometimes called Bull's Eye) It helps everyone sequence (or know what next to do) to accomplish their goals. Helps the bodies 12 different systems to work in unison and be in balance. Bull's eye (Like tiger's eye)has a soothing effect and can be used for grounding and stabilizing. Helps to keep you on focus and enhances attention span.

Some people are usually excellent employees, if they do not get distracted by all the other things going on in their world. As business owners they can get MORE easily drawn away by events that have nothing to do with their occupation. Bull's Eye helps to keep them focused by the energy of this High Iron content stone. Helps them to get into and hold "the ZONE".

Bulls Eye can help you to exactly focus on what is essential. You can look at something with your eyesight or you can look at something with a microscope and see more deeply. The red tiger's eye can help you see into a situation. It can also cause you to go too deep. If you already are happy with how you perceive and see what is going on... then Bull's Eye may cause you to over-focus. Looking at a crack in a coffee cup to0 closely can make it look like a canyon (requiring an expedition) rather than a spot of glue.

The First Position...

... "Zero in and go for it" was the energy that you brought in with you as a baby, If you look back you will probably see that your family went through a period of the most productive time, shortly after you were born.

The Second Position...

… You were probably a little obsessive when you were a toddler and young child... didn't like to be disturbed while you were doing something. Probably didn't take nap well unless you fell asleep where you were. It is probably difficult for you even now to walk away from a project until it's done.

The Third Position...

… Bull's Eye in this position tells me that you were very focused and good at whatever held your interest when you were in school. If friends were your interest, you had a lot of those. If sports was your interest, then you probably set records, If homework was your interest, then you probably got a lot of "A's".

The Fourth Position...

... Tiger Eye Red here tells me that you had a target for your life, You may have started at 16, 18, 20 or 25 but, when you started, that was your switch to an adult or non-childlike path. Things came to you, and other things dropped away, because they added to or took away from that target.

The Fifth Position...

... Your focus is shifting and you do not have to feel bad because of this change, it is necessary for the growth of all those around you and everyone involved in this change.

The Sixth Position...?

... Now is the time to make a point, start doing the thing that can appear to leave a legacy or mark that you were here and the universe will support you in it. Move now, change now, start now... All of All is behind you.

Tourmaline, Black

Is great for overall grounding, really good for putting stops into materials with a talisman and is a super tool when doing a healing crystal or stone layout. Stabilizes and/or enhances electromagnetic fields. Calms the angry heart and reduces stress. Makes the spiritual body alert. Purifies the energetic environment.

Black tourmaline's other name is Schorl (named after a small town in Germany prior to 1400 AD) and is a very interesting material. Because it is pyroelectric, it creates current as the temperature changes, then the charge dissipates as it stabilizes in temperature. Would make an interesting powered talisman for that reason.

For over 2500 years, the **Sinhalese** healers and teachers used *turamali* (their name for black tourmaline and meant ash stone) to pull infection & inflammation out of one of their tribe... I'm sure it is just a coincidence that modern science has discoverede that carbon (ash) will do that exact same thing. (http://www.ncbi.nlm.nih.gov/pubmed/9484098) Different ancient healing modalities would use black tourmaline worn under the nose or around the neck to help with breathing disorders... carbon filters are used by the military and to cure "sick" buildings. (http://www.airgle.com/blog/air-purifiers/charcoal-air-purifier-charcoal-filter-chemical-air-purifier/)

The First Position...
... When people held you as an infant they got a chance to think about all the things they had done correctly and so, you got the chance to help people feel "right" about themselves.

The Second Position...
... You were probably a good little helper to everyone around you when you were a small child. A willingness and ability to help or serve is a gift.

The Third Position...

... It's easy to hand a capable person "things to do". You probably found yourself with a lot of chores as a teenager and/or helped your friends with things they had to do. This may also have translated into adulthood with an ability to take on a project and get it done.

The Fourth Position...

... You may have gotten tired of handling other peoples' stuff or simply rolled into your own responsibilities without much "right of passage" or fan fare. However, being capable doesn't mean you should be handling other peoples' situations.

The Fifth Position...

... There are certain things one gains from being the person everyone can come to, but there are also anchors involved. The balance for you now is to shift those responsibilities onto the people you have been handling life for and to free yourself up to address your core and your needs.

The Sixth Position...?

... You may feel uncomfortable for a while (if this hasn't already begun). Temperature and temperaments are going to fluctuate, but each time that happens it is giving you power to move forward toward your interests.

Turquoise...

...Most of the native American tribes used the Aztec word *Teoxihuitl* . It helps open the throat chakra for better communication and assists in better hearing. Gain understanding and focus as well. King Tut, Roman Emperors, the priests of Delphi, and the Mayan and Aztec rulers all wore turquoise for the power and insight it gave them. Will polish and brighten your charisma. Has been a token of wealth for thousands of years and will brighten your path toward prosperity as well.

Turquoise has Copper , Aluminum, Phosphorus, hydrogen and oxygen (formula $CuAl6(PO4)4(OH)8•4(H2O)$. Copper is used to stimulate communication in the digital, physical and emotional realms, Aluminum can affect brain activity in very positive ways for memory and other mental functions, Phosphorus is important for self image and other emotional support areas. While hydrogen and oxygen are import for sustained and vibrant life.

Turquoise is considered to be a cryptocrystaline deposit and has only, very, rarely produce a single gem grade crystal (one was found in Lynch Station, Campbell County, Virginia, USA). from around the world the color ranges from pale blue to hunter green and can be found with a hardness of window glass (5-6) to that of baby powder. Most of the deposits in the American southwest are very porous or flaky so, even in ancient time some of it was blended with cactus or Agave nectar then heated to harden. That is where it gets the small nodule (or bubbly) look that turquoise is so well known for. Only on the exterior of a deposit does it look like that.

The First Position...

... When people held you as a baby they would find themselves thinking and (better) feeling a world of possibilities, not just for you, but for themselves also.

The Second Position...

... You were probably a very friendly child; getting to know everyone in the neighborhood or at a party was pretty easy for you as a child. You still seem to meet people pretty well.

The Third Position...

... You were probably a popular teenager, if not the most popular certainly well known within the group you ran with. Maybe even found making money wasn't hard for you.

The Fourth Position...

... You were tired of waiting and wanted your own way; world and wealth is the reason you left your family and friends behind to strike out into the world. Some of those friends may have returned to your world because they saw value in having you around.

The Fifth Position...

... You are an accomplished person by the world's standards, but did you leave or drop something along the way? You can win the world over with your words but, did you talk right past what was important?

The Sixth Position...?

... Those things that you have been working on are beginning to bud and will bear fruit very soon. Recognition will be yours also.

Turquoise can be found many places in the world.

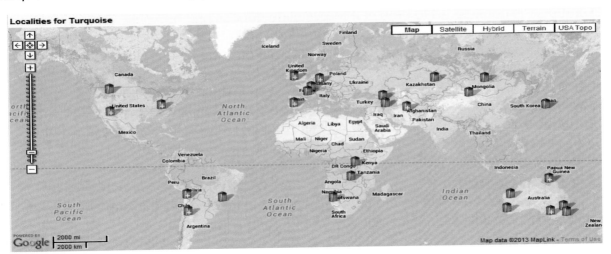

Unakite

Rediscovered in the Unakas mountains of North Carolina and named unakite by the people that discovered it. Ancient Cherokee healers would use this stone to pull someone back into a more balanced life. Good for the emotions, mental stability, spiritual integrity and helps to break physical addictions.

Because it is a settled and hardened composite of other known stones (pink orthoclase, epidote and quartz), it has a wonderful base of elements; Potassium, Calcium, Aluminum, Iron, Silicon, Hydrogen, Oxygen. It's formula for the soup mother nature cooked up would look something like $Ca_2K(Fe,Al)Al_3(SiO_4)(Si_2O_7)O_8(OH)$. So, this is an enhancer of the emotional, mental and spiritual body while being a balancer for the physical body. If someone is obsessive/compulsive, stressed, worry-some, very talkative... etc. this would work within the four bodies to bring them back into line.

The First Position...
... You are a peace bringer and people felt very at ease while holding you as an infant Peace has many interpretations, one of which is to be at rest or ease. You have the gift of making people be comfortable around you which can be very useful as a healer or detective.

The Second Position...
... You were probably one of those very good toddlers that people thank the heavens for. You were not just thoughtful but were very much into your own discovery and therefore didn't need (or want) much supervision.

The Third Position...
... Many people may have thought you were shy when you were a teenager. Introspection isn't shy. You were thinking, thoughtful, contemplative and I'm sure many other teenagers thought you were cool to know.

The Fourth Position...
... You wanted to find your own level or to create some degree of balance/regularity within your world. A regular regiment was your hope and you may have left your family and childhood by joining the military or some other strict college or life program.

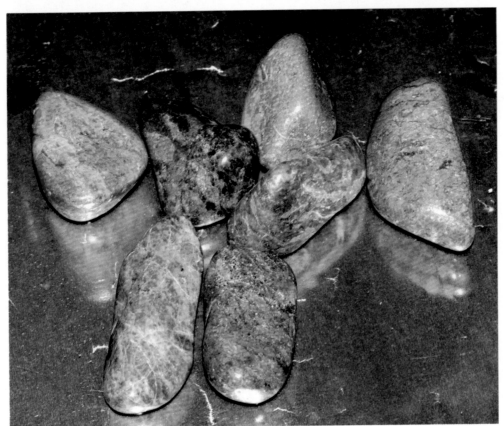

The Fifth Position...

… This is a time that you need to examine the four parts of yourself (physical, emotional, mental and spiritual) and see what and where reality lives for you. This is more about reminding you to check your path than to tell you to make any change. It's like making sure you are on the course you want so you don't end up where you didn't intend.

The Sixth Position...?

... You are headed toward a new level emotionally, mentally and spiritually. You have done a lot of prep work and now are going to move up the incline of a new experience. If you let go of old assumptions and ideas easily you will build up momentum to quickly ascend to that higher better place. If you hang onto the old, the climb will be much slower and more effort will be needed.

Anystone

The "Anystone" is an awesome stone of your own choosing. The stones listed in this book are enough to do a very respectable Ancient Stone Reading. Now, you should add your stones to it. The tradition is that the next and subsequent stones will come to you when you are ready for them. It is also tradition that when you receive this stone from nature or from a friend, that you give something in return for it. Isn't it nice that we have a convenient exchange called currency? You can get more from your local store and give them currency in exchange.

However, it doesn't have to only be a stone. I have carried a piece of beach glass that my friend Donna gave me after she and her husband returned from a vacation.

Here is how you do it when you have a material you want to add to your reading bag. Look at this token or anystone that you have. Write down three or four descriptive words that help you to know what that token means to you. Then turn those into sentences that more fully express this. Now let it set with the description for a day or so. Then come back to it and see if you want to change anything. If you do change anything, repeat the last step.

Then, when you are satisfied with your descriptions, work it into your reading.

The First Position...
... This position describes what you would see if you were to apply this token or anystone to a newly born infant and/or a child up to about five years of age. Write that down.

The Second Position...
… Read your description again. If you were to apply this token or anystone to a child from six years to 13 years of age, what would you say this meant for them?

The Third Position...
… Read your description again. If you were to apply this token or anystone to a person in her teenage years up to just before she was to leave home, what would you see?

The Fourth Position...
… This one is a little tougher—maybe you want to meditate on it, but then again, you might just give it a shot. Read your description again. Apply this token or anystone to anytime he or she leaves home or to any event that is associated with the young adult years.

The Fifth Position...

... This one is tougher yet. Read your description again. Apply this token or anystone to events in the person's near past to now and to the outcomes she is bringing with the energy that personifies her now.

The Sixth Position...?

... Read your description again. If you were to apply this token or anystone to someone's future, what would that be?

My grandmother had a bag of stones, shells, and wood that she taught me with, and I carry at least 50 stones in my bag at all times. However you can do an accurate reading with as few as 25 stones. To help you make this *your* Ancient Stone Reading, I will include a page that you can photocopy and use when you find an important anystone or token. If you know what the stone is, do no change the definition of one of the ones I gave you, it could create a "misread situation" whenever that stone is drawn.

Item description:

The First Position...

The Second Position...

The Third Position...

The Fourth Position...

The Fifth Position...

The Sixth Position...?

An Example of the Use of the Anystone section.

I was given a piece of BEACHGLASS from the Caribbean by a dear friend (Donna) who owned the Hidden Meadow Healing Center near Barringer, Maine. She gave me this piece after she and her husband had returned from their vacation.

This piece means FUN to me... Maybe because I would like to have Fun In the Caribbean.

Beach glass may have completely different meanings to many people but, the point is: How does this beach glass appeal to me? Anything like man made glass has a very neutral energy and is only what we assign to it.

Item description:

a piece of BEACHGLASS from the Caribbean.. Means FUN, FUN, FUN and fun in the sun.

The First Position...

You were a fun diversion for anyone that held you as a baby.

The Second Position...

You were a very active toddler and loved discovery in your early childhood. The discovery of Fun was your guiding light, at this time.

The Third Position...

Too much fun isn't possible... You were probably involved in groups, sports, or other activities when you were in middle or high *school*.

The Fourth Position...

You were taking life too seriously in your teenage years and left home looking to attract or create a little fun in your life.

The Fifth Position...

Start looking for where the fun can fit into your life. Time to celebrate is right around the corner. Make sure you are ready to accept it when it comes.

The Sixth Position...

Fun is coming soon. Find it and enjoy it.

Talismans and other ornaments of stone

The other day, someone asked me, "What is a talisman?" A talisman is a surface to which other stones and objects are affixed to create a response. Sounds like a motherboard in a computer, doesn't it? Well, that is a way to understand it. A talisman can be as small as a wristwatch or as large as a stadium. It is generally the size of a pendant to the size of a plate, but I have made them the size of a car. There are powered talismans and unpowered talismans. The power of a talisman can be like a nuclear reaction or the power of a pocket watch. Unpowered talismans can float on a pond or have the impact of a landslide. A talisman can look pretty hanging around your neck or on a blouse as a pendant while healing the bearer or a whole community, or affecting the path of an entire government.

Talismans have been made out wood, metal, and stone, have been discovered in the caves of ancient civilizations, and have been constructed on the sites of our most modern structures (without the architects, builders, or construction crew knowing they were building one). So my best description of a talisman is "a base in which component elements are connected or mounted for the purpose of having or creating an effect on an energy field or area."

Although you might appreciate a piece of elemental magic in the form of a prosperity talisman that you or anyone else can build to help your business or yourself. You can get the material to create it from anywhere... or you can get the materials from the store where you bought this book or from my website: (shamansdream.net).

To power the grid of stones get a slab of REAL granite... you can usually get a granite tile from any big hardware store. Granite has a magnetic radiation that is not hurtful but helpful to people. Most banks, lawyers offices, medical and government offices have granite as their foundation or floor tiles. I teach about this in some of my workshops and about the following list of stones. The information is also coming out in book form. I'm not going to repeat the

workshop or book information here, but I will point out that there are important elements of prosperity in each of these stones so do not leave any of them out. If you don't want to follow the spell, you don't have to, but, you know what happens when you half do a spell...

You will need to place in a circle on the tile one each of: Malachite, Pyrite, Jade, Mystic Topaz, Diamond (can be Herkimer Diamond), Shatukite, Peridot, Emerald (can be rough), Rainbow Obsidian, Ruby (can be rough), and Danburite. Now lay an inexpensive gold necklace (better is better) as a slalom by each stone and in between the stone next to it. DO NOT COMPLETELY WRAP AROUND ANY STONE. Then take a silver necklace and wrap it around the outside of the circle of stones and gold but on the slab of granite.

A fork in the path...

Now that you have come to the end of our little bit of sharing and passing of the talking stick, I wish to point out a chance to embrace what you have learned in a professional way. You can take what is in this book and make yourself professionally good at it—in other words, not just make a living, but be worthy of other people's support as their counselor and reader. If you would like to proceed along this financially rewarding path, then you will need to practice. Tell your family and friends what you are trying to do and that you would like to practice with them. (And you might remind them that they will benefit the most from your honed skills as encouragement for them to give you permission to practice on them, in the same way a masseuse practices on his friends and family). As you move forward with your talent you will increase in ability the same way an athlete increases in ability: Your strength and stamina will grow at a rate equal to support the growth of your insight.

If you are already an experienced reader, then it is simply a matter of learning what the stones represent and their different meanings inside of the spreads that you use.

You can also continue through to other levels in the work toward being a Stoneman or Stonewoman. This can be a spiritual path as well as a professional one, but it isn't required that you be both. You may incorporate many of the teachings of my ancestors in your work but in order to be recognized for your position of growth there are certain requirements to be met. If you feel that you are called to walk the Stone Path, you would need to commit to a regimen of time and effort to accomplish it, the same as you would for any endeavor where you would benefit educationally, occupationally, and financially. Just as in becoming a doctor, lawyer, therapist, or counselor, the main ingredient in all of these efforts is the intentional fortitude to see it through to the end.

TO WHAT END?

You can polish this and become a <u>stone reader</u>;

The next level is a <u>Talisman maker</u>, the point at which you begin to learn the magic and the mystery surrounding our interdependency on the stones we have all around us–knowing about the 168 stones that can absolutely change the world, and how you can make that happen for yourself and the world around you. This is a great level for anyone who wants to or has made jewelry or works with beads. Certificate available.

A <u>Stone Investigator</u> is the next step. These individuals are geologists, priests, scientists, and earth stewards–individuals who will either buy or make (with training) all the equipment to test all that we have stated. A Stone Investigator proves to herself and then to the world not just the body connection, but our spiritual, emotional, and mental affiliation to all the stones, minerals, and crystals..., and therefore proves our interdependence with our planet itself. Certificate and Ordination available when this level is completed.

A <u>Stone Healer</u> takes the knowledge of the ancients and the new research of the Stone Investigator and applies the knowledge of anatomy and physiology with the understanding of how the body responds to certain stones, minerals, and/or the frequency of gems and crystals and comes up with a verifiable treatment plan for an individual or animal. A stone healer will have an understanding at the end of this coursework that acknowledges more than physical treatment: it will also take into consideration the individual person's emotional, mental, and spiritual connection to disease and healing. Certificate and Ordination available when this level is completed

A <u>Stone Facilitator</u> understands the previous modalities well enough to assist and/or supervise those that are doing the work for the Stone man/woman who is in charge of this group. By the time someone earns this title, he will understand all aspects on an administrative level. He will also be able to work with individuals, couples, families, companies, and corporations in a counseling or pastoral capacity. He will be able to help the any person heal emotionally, mentally, and spiritually on an exceptionally deep level. Certificate available.

The <u>Stone Man or Woman</u> is a title that is bestowed on an individual by the existing stone men

or women when the candidate has demonstrated his or her ability to manage, coordinate, and build a community. The individual must be willing to accept the responsibility that goes with the title legally, practically, and spiritually. There are two people who are trying to work toward your goal of you being ready for the title and its responsibilities: You and the stone man/woman you are working with will have to convince the other stone men and stone women of your readiness. After you have achieved the level of Stone Facilitator, you must declare your intention. Then you will be given additional coursework and studies to prepare you. You are not required to share the same spiritual belief that your Stone Man or Stone Woman has for any part of this educational process... You can be a Buddhist, Baptist, Muslim, Wicca, Pagan, Shamanic, Naturalist, or one of the many tribal beliefs. The science behind what we do is solid as... Stone. Your belief in it isn't required for it to work. Certificate available and plaque presented

Thank You for allowing me to be of service, and a part of your path.

StoneMan,
TL Harris

Throughout time our species has sought to place value on metals, minerals, crystals and gems.

Science would have you believe that it's because we are attracted to "sparkly". That may also be true. However almost none of the stones sparkle in there natural form. So, why would we have found it useful to carry these around in our medicine pouch or wear them around our neck? For the last 10,000 years our race has sought to find a spiritual connection in things we can not touch, taste or feel (ie: God and Heaven). Science proved that our species has been around for at least 200,000 years. Maybe the ancients tapped the magic of the stones because they understood the mystery.

The stone you are attracted to (either for your alter or for your jewelery box) says something about what you need and what you are attracting to yourself... ***Learn more about the stones and yourself from this book.***

T L Harris was a corporate consultant and psychic for many years.

Then a 40 day and 40 night experience in the middle of Maine that was intense emotionally, mentally, spiritually and physically … "and then" being struck by lighting twice (not on the same day) these experiences caused him to turn away from his long corporate and financial pursuits to a life of service.... He brings to you a desire to be of service, from the words he received during his experience, and the mainstream experience to help you apply it. He frequently shares his insight over the phone with international and corporate clients around the globe and he shares this same insight with people who read this book. His greatest wish is to help you find grace for your path or growth in your business.

Love & Light...

Additional Information about TL Harris' other classes and books can be found at www.shamansdream.net